KEY TO SYMBOLS

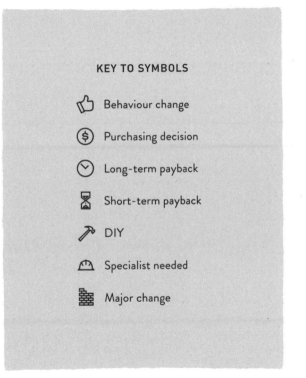

Behaviour change

Purchasing decision

Long-term payback

Short-term payback

DIY

Specialist needed

Major change

CONTENTS

HOW TO REDUCE YOUR CARBON FOOTPRINT

PRACTICAL WAYS TO MAKE A REAL DIFFERENCE

ELLEN TOUT

WATKINS
Sharing Wisdom Since 1893

How To Reduce Your Carbon Footprint
Ellen Tout

First published in the UK and USA in 2022 by
Watkins, an imprint of Watkins Media Limited
Unit 11, Shepperton House, 83–93 Shepperton Road
London N1 3DF

enquiries@watkinspublishing.com

Commissioning Editor: Ella Chappell
Managing Editor: Daniel Culver
Managing Designer: Karen Smith
Designer: Alice Coleman
Production: Uzma Taj

A CIP record for this book is available from the British Library

ISBN: 978-1-78678-648-7 (Paperback)
ISBN: 978-1-78678-649-4 (eBook)

10 9 8 7 6 5 4 3 2 1

Typeset in Brandon Grotesque
Printed in the United Kingdom by TJ Books Ltd

www.watkinspublishing.com

INTRODUCTION

We've been hearing about carbon footprints for a while – in the news, at school and from scientists. The concept isn't new but until recent years, your carbon footprint might not have felt so tangible. The Covid-19 pandemic and subsequent lockdowns, COP events, Extinction Rebellion protests and IPCC reports, to name just a few examples, have shown that the climate crisis is a very real factor in our daily lives.

This introduction, and entire book, could be a series of terrifying statistics, quotes and scenarios. But I don't think that would help. If you're reading this book, the chances are that you are already, at least somewhat, aware of the challenges facing our planet, communities and wildlife. Instead, this book gives you the tools to make evidence-based changes – some of them being little tweaks to your daily routine, others being bigger DIY or gardening projects, and everything in between.

For the last five years, I have written about sustainability as a journalist and author. This started as one single page in a magazine, but the more I wrote, the more demand there was for it. Writing about these issues made me feel more empowered. I was doing something about it. It also showed me the many, many amazing people also doing something about it: from interviewing the founder of my local zero-waste shop, to speaking at vegan markets about waste-free cooking; or receiving emails from readers keen to make changes, and finding community groups cleaning beaches, organising rallies, and saving green spaces.

The fact that almost every area of human activity contributes to our carbon footprint might sound like an overwhelming problem. But this means that there is scope to reduce our footprint in every aspect of our lives. Every single little positive step each of us takes does make a difference – it has a ripple effect, inspiring more people, sparking more small tweaks and adding up to real change. While many of those in power are failing us, we can also vote with our actions, sending a message to businesses, brands and governments that we demand better.

This book is packed full of changes you could make. These are suggestions and advice. Dip in and out, try one a day, week, or month. Take control for yourself but don't feel that you need to check every single one off. Doing this should not feel like a burden – make it fun, be creative and slow down. Remember the quote by zero-waste chef Anne-Marie Bonneau: "We don't need a handful of people doing it (zero-waste) perfectly. We need millions of people doing it imperfectly."

WHAT ACTUALLY IS A CARBON FOOTPRINT?

The phrase carbon footprint may not be a new concept to you – but it's not always easy to know where to start when trying to measure or reduce it. A carbon footprint is the amount of carbon dioxide (CO_2) emitted as a direct or indirect result of an activity. Almost everything we do results in carbon emissions – from breathing to travelling, warming our homes or buying food.

Human and other forms of life impacting the environment by emitting carbon dioxide is a pattern as old as the hills; life itself has always depended on and affected the planet's carbon cycle. All organic matter contains carbon, and this is released and reabsorbed in a continuous flow. What's new is the scale of the impact humans are having, and the imbalance it's causing in the biosphere.

THE POWER IS IN YOUR HANDS – AND THEIRS

Around the world, thousands of local authorities, governments and administrations have formally declared a climate emergency, and are debating how best to regulate emissions. But many of them are not doing anywhere near enough, and shockingly, just 100 companies are responsible for 71% of global emissions.

While businesses and those in power are starting to wake up, there are so many things we can each do as individuals to reduce our own carbon footprints – in the everyday actions described in this book and in our wider sphere of influence as consumers, voters and global citizens. Avoid polluting companies, write to your MP/ senator or local councillor, join rallies and protests, attend a beach clean, support greener companies, chat to your neighbours, and try some of the many changes in this book. Imagine the difference each of us can make when we do this together.

Thank you,
Ellen Tout
@ellen_tout

Every 2 minutes the sun gives the Earth more energy than we use in a year.

 Renewable energy sources provided more electricity to the UK than fossil fuels for the first time in 2019.

 Installing a smart meter could help your household save at least 5% in gas consumption.

 40% of UK emissions come from households. Energy production, mainly through burning fossil fuels, accounts for ¾ of global greenhouse gas emissions.

RENEWABLE ENERGY

However much you streamline your energy use, you're still going to need *some* power. By taking advantage of the growing availability of renewable energy, you'll keep the carbon footprint of your energy use as low as possible.

⊙ **BRING ME SUNSHINE** Photovoltaic (PV) technology, also known as solar, harnesses energy from the sun's rays to create electricity or heat water. Modern PV panels require only daylight (not necessarily direct sunlight) to generate electricity and so can still generate some power on a cloudy day. Prices are falling and installing solar panels or tiles on your roof or walls will provide free electricity to power your home – in fact it could save you up to £230 a year on your energy bills. If that's too much of an investment, try out one of the many pieces of solar equipment – from mobile phone chargers to radios – now on the market. You may never need to buy another battery.

⊙ **WINDS OF CHANGE** Domestic wind turbines can be free-standing or smaller turbines can even be installed on your roof. You could use a small turbine to charge a battery system in your home, which could cut your electricity bill by a third and your household carbon footprint by up to half a tonne (1,100lb) of CO_2 a year. If you produce an

WHY DO WE NEED RENEWABLE ENERGY? By 2030, 42% of the average household's carbon footprint is expected to come from heating and 9% from electricity. Low-carbon electricity could reduce emissions by 79%. Each of our homes plays a huge role in meeting emissions targets and tackling the climate crisis.

As supplies of fossil fuels become scarcer, we could see energy bills rocket – in 2022 UK prices rose by a record 50% due to gas shortages – and supplies are likely to become a growing source of political tension.

Renewable energy sources are an increasingly viable alternative. Not only are they carbon neutral (emitting negligible CO_2 into the atmosphere), they have numerous other advantages. They rely on free fuel, so running costs are low and predictable, avoiding the economic chaos of fuel price fluctuations. They're abundantly available worldwide, and are far less vulnerable to terrorist attack than conventional energy sources.

Renewable energy sources are becoming rapidly more available, especially wind and solar power. The costs of these and other renewables are therefore falling as technologies develop, manufacturing becomes automated and economies of scale are achieved.

If progress in this sector continues at current rates, up to a billion people could use renewable energy in the next decade, and renewables could account for a third to a half of global energy production by 2050.

excess, you could even sell it to the national grid. Alternatively, sign up to a wind energy tariff (see column opposite). You could buy shares in a new windfarm or support a community windpower scheme. It's likely to be a solid investment.

TAKE TO THE WAVES The energy held in the oceans' waves, currents, tides and temperature differentials can be tapped for human use. Most of the technologies in these areas are still at the experimental stage, but several significant and successful tidal-power installations are already in action. Australia, Portugal and Scotland are among a growing list of countries investing in ocean-energy technologies. Find out more, and if you're in favour of this carbon-neutral power source, support any proposals for installations in your local area.

GO TO GROUND The ground absorbs and stores heat from the sun. Ground-source heat pumps (see p.24) involve embedding a network of pipes beneath the ground to harness this natural warmth, which can then be used to heat, or – in a reverse process – to cool, buildings. Similarly, air-source heat pumps absorb heat from the outside air to heat your home and water.

($) POWER PLANTS Biomass produced from organic materials, either directly from plants or indirectly from industrial or agricultural by-products (such as manure or household waste), has huge potential as a renewable energy source. For example, it can be used to heat your home or as a motor fuel, although there are limitations to the land available to grow virgin crops. Although by-products release carbon dioxide when burned, this is considerably less than fossil fuels. "Green gas", which is vegan and made from grass cuttings, is also gradually being introduced.

($) DAM IT Hydropower is the biggest source of renewable energy and creates 16% of the world's electricity. However, droughts and unpredictable weather could pose difficulties for hydropower. Large dams have also been criticized for their impact on the local environment and community.

($) POWER TO THE PEOPLE Community energy schemes create renewable energy locally, putting the profits back into the community, powering local homes and helping people have more control over their energy. You can even invest in or start your own community energy scheme.

SIGN UP FOR GREEN POWER

Even if you can't generate your own energy at home, you can still meet your household's electricity needs using renewable power by signing up to one of the growing number of companies supplying energy from renewable sources such as wind energy. Although all suppliers deliver their energy via the national grid, check that yours is actually investing in building more renewable capacity rather than simply offering a "green" tariff (which can be quite meaningless), and your home will be participating in the global push to more renewable energy.

WORK WITH THE SUN

Traditionally, buildings were designed to take advantage of their local surroundings and climate. Thick walls would keep the summer heat out and retain warmth in the winter. In hot climates, buildings were painted light colours to reflect the sun's heat. Windows were relatively small to keep out the sun, and shady, leafy courtyards helped keep the interior cool. In cold climates, buildings were painted dark colours to absorb the sun's heat, and south-facing windows were larger to take advantage of the sun's warmth.

With the advent of central heating and air conditioning, the principles of passive heating and cooling were often sidelined, but now many modern architects are returning to this timeless wisdom.

SUN AND SHADE

Instead of relying entirely on mechanical heating and cooling, use sun exposure and shading to keep your home at a comfortable temperature.

TRAIN VINES up trellises on the hottest side of the house. Keep the trellis at least 15cm (6in) from the wall to provide a buffer of cool air.

PLANT TREES to provide summer shade and block winter winds. If you go for deciduous trees, they will provide the additional benefit of letting through the sun in winter.

FIT AWNINGS or movable roof overhangs to block out hot summer sun, but allow it in during the winter. Light-coloured curtains and blinds can also help reduce heat gain. In winter, keep them open during the day to let sunlight in.

PAINT YOUR HOME a light colour if you live in a warm climate, or a dark colour if you live in a cold climate. Special reflective, or absorbent, roof coatings are also available.

Your house doesn't need to be facing due south to enjoy passive solar heat gain. Buildings facing within 30° of due south still get 90% of the sun's benefit.

 Another way to use plants to minimize heat gain is to plant a "green roof" (see p.71). A green roof can reduce a building's heating and cooling costs by up to 50%.

 Shading can reduce indoor temperatures by as much as 11°C (52°F), minimizing the need for mechanical cooling.

As much as half the energy used in homes and in commercial buildings goes into heating and cooling.

In the sun, black surfaces can be up to 40°C hotter than white or silver ones

Dark-coloured exteriors absorb 70% to 90% of the radiant solar energy striking a building.

When fitting draught-proofing, allow adequate ventilation, especially if you have a solid-fuel fire, a gas fire or a boiler with an open flue.

 As well as preventing warm air escaping during winter, draught-proofing can stop hot air coming in during summer, reducing your need for air con.

Studies have found that improving the air-tightness of dwellings can yield energy savings of 15% to 30%.

 Draught-proofing the average home effectively can cut its annual CO_2 emissions by around 150kg (330lb).

 Installing glass doors around a fireplace can reduce heat loss up the chimney by 50%.

DRAUGHTS

Sitting in a draught isn't just uncomfortable, it's also incredibly wasteful – 20% of the heat lost from the average home seeps out through unsealed gaps.

DO A HOME DRAUGHT AUDIT Hold a lit candle next to window and door frames (ideally on a windy day). Wherever it flickers, there's a draught that needs to be plugged.

EXCLUDE DRAUGHTS Stop heat sneaking out and make your home more comfortable by fixing draught excluders (see right) around doors, windows and letter boxes. Fill gaps between skirting boards and the floor with silicone sealant or wooden beading.

KEEP DOORS CLOSED when the heating's on to stop draughts running through the house.

PLUG YOUR CHIMNEY with a "chimney balloon". This device sits about 30cm (1ft) up inside the chimney, and stops warm air escaping up the flue. Just remember to remove it when you light a fire.

THE INS AND OUTS OF DRAUGHT-PROOFING
Draught-proofing is an easy, cost-effective way to stop unwanted airflows into and out of your house and reduce your heating (or cooling) bills. Most draught-proofing materials are readily available from DIY stores, and are relatively easy to fit. They fall into three main categories:

- compression seals: self-adhesive foam, rubber or tube strips for use around windows and swinging doors
- wiper seals: less flexible brush or sprung strips for use around sash windows and sliding doors; they create less friction than compression seals
- caulking: usually a silicone rubber sealant (but can also be made from other materials, such as wooden beading) – used for filling gaps.

WHAT'S THE POINT OF INSULATION?

Good insulation plays a key role in reducing a building's carbon footprint. It keeps the heat in during the winter and out during the summer, reducing the need for energy-intensive heating and cooling. Around half of the heat lost from a typical home escapes through the walls and loft, so insulating these areas is a priority. Floor insulation, double-glazing, draught-proofing (see pp.18–19), and tank and pipe insulation (see p.23) also play important roles in regulating your home's temperature. As well as making your home more efficient to run, insulation also provides less obvious benefits, such as keeping noise out (or in) and helping to prevent mould forming on walls and ceilings (condensation being caused, in part, by fluctuations in temperature).

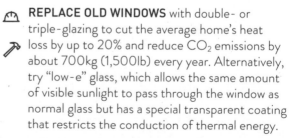

INSULATION

While it may not turn as many heads as a solar panel or wind turbine, installing decent insulation is one of the most significant things you can do to reduce your home's carbon footprint.

 INSULATE YOUR LOFT to avoid losing up to a third of your heating through the roof. In cold climates make sure the insulation's at least 270mm (10½in) thick to get good results. This traps heat rising from below, prevents the sun baking your home in the summer and could cut your home's annual CO_2 emissions by up to 1.5 tonnes (3,300lb).

 LOOK FOR A HIGH R-VALUE when shopping for insulating material. This is a measure of its thermal resistance – the greater the R-value, the more effective it'll be at resisting heat flow into the building in summer, and out of it in winter.

REPLACE OLD WINDOWS with double- or triple-glazing to cut the average home's heat loss by up to 20% and reduce CO_2 emissions by about 700kg (1,500lb) every year. Alternatively, try "low-e" glass, which allows the same amount of visible sunlight to pass through the window as normal glass but has a special transparent coating that restricts the conduction of thermal energy.

If everyone in the UK topped up their loft insulation to 270mm (10½in), the energy saving would pay the fuel bills of over 640,000 households.

Uninsulated curtains can cut heat loss through windows by a third, and insulated curtains can reduce it by half.

Natural insulating materials require up to 10 times less energy to produce than synthetic materials such as fibreglass.

Replacing six largeish single-pane windows with double-glazing could avoid 4,500kg (10,000lb) of CO_2 and save more than £200 each year.

Insulating under your ground floor could cut your home's heat loss by up to 25%.

Made from recycled denim jeans, combined with post-industrial denim and cotton, denim insulation is pleasant to work with and highly insulating.

VERTICAL HOLD

40% of the heat lost from an uninsulated home escapes through the walls. The best way to insulate exterior walls depends on whether they are of cavity or solid construction:

- To insulate cavity walls, contractors drill a small hole in the wall and inject insulating material to fill the cavity. This reduces heat loss by up to 60% and could cut the average home's CO_2 emissions by a tonne (2,200lb) every year.
- Clad solid walls with a decorative weather-proof insulating treatment. On a 3-bedroom semi-detached house this could save nearly 2.5 tonnes (5,500lb) of CO_2 a year, paying for itself in 5–6 years.
- Or insulate from the inside, using ready-made insulation/plasterboard laminates, or wooden battens in-filled with insulation and covered with plasterboard, or flexible insulating lining.

This minimizes heat loss during cold weather and heat gain during hot weather. If you're on a budget, opt for secondary glazing panels, which are a less permanent, but reasonably effective, alternative to new windows, or apply an adhesive insulating film to the glass.

 CLOSE CURTAINS OR BLINDS each evening. This can be as effective at keeping warmth in as fitting an extra layer of glazing – particularly if your curtains have thick thermal linings.

INSULATE UNDER YOUR FLOOR, and seal gaps between floorboards if they are uncovered.

GET HELP Many local authorities offer grants or special rates on loft and cavity-wall insulation.

DO WHAT COMES NATURALLY Invest in insulating products derived from natural or recycled materials, such as cork, repurposed denim or hemp.

BOILER

Heating space and water accounts for a significant proportion of our homes' energy requirements. The type of boiler you have and the way you use it will play a key role in reducing your home's carbon footprint.

ALL PART OF THE SERVICE Get the most out of your boiler by having it serviced annually. If it's more than 10 years old, it's almost certainly pretty inefficient, and ready for an upgrade.

GET A CONDENSING BOILER All modern boilers are now condensing models, which are much more efficient than older boilers. They use a heat exchanger to recycle some of the heat in the flue gases, which would otherwise be lost. Such boilers are about 90% efficient (compared with 60–70% for a conventional 1980s boiler), and so can cut your gas bills by 20–30%.

LAG YOUR PIPES AND BOILER and cut your home's CO_2 emissions by up to 400kg (900lb) per year. Make sure that the insulation's at least 2.5cm (1in) thick on pipes and 7.5cm (3in) thick on the boiler (you could even use an old duvet as lagging). Your investment should be recouped within 6 months.

RENEWABLE HEAT SOURCES

Even the most efficient oil- or gas-fired boiler will emit a significant amount of CO_2. Heating systems that are powered by renewable energy sources offer a low- or no-carbon alternative.

- Solar water-heating systems capture the sun's energy shining onto south-facing collector panels. Depending on the climate you live in, this type of system could meet a large proportion of your hot water needs.
- Common in Scandinavia, biomass-powered Combined Heat and Power (CHP) systems involve burning waste wood chips or other biomass fuel at a neighbourhood plant to generate electricity. The heat produced is distributed to local homes to provide heating and hot water. This combined process almost doubles the efficiency of energy use.

- As long as the fuel comes from a well-managed forest, wood-burning stoves are a renewable and carbon-neutral energy source. Traditional fireplaces are generally 10–30% efficient, while modern stoves are up to 85% efficient. They use wood offcuts, pellets made from compacted sawdust, wood chips, bark, agricultural crop waste, waste paper, spent coffee grounds or other organic materials.
- Ground-source geothermal heat pumps harness the heat from beneath your feet. They run fluid through a network of collector pipes buried in the ground. The fluid absorbs the earth's natural warmth, which is then converted into superheated gas to warm your home. Geothermal systems can also cool your home in the summer. Similarly, air-source heat pumps absorb heat from the outside air to heat your home and water.

KEEP HEAT LOCAL If you're installing a new boiler, situate it close to where the hot water will be used most often to avoid heat loss on long journeys around the house.

INSTALL A COMBINATION BOILER, which burns energy only when you actually need hot water. They cut out standby heat loss (up to 4% per hour) and can halve the cost of heating water.

GO IT ALONE If you're not lucky enough to live in an area with a neighbourhood CHP system (see p.23), you could invest in a gas-fired domestic model. Although these are powered by a fossil fuel, they can reduce energy use by up to 25%.

TURN TO THE SUN If you live in an area of seasonal sun (such as the northern United States), a solar water-heating system should provide all your hot water over the summer and about a third of your needs the rest of the year.

Installing a solar water heater could cut your water-heating bills by up to 80%.

⚠️ Heating accounts for roughly 53% of what you spend in a year on energy bills.

✅ Geothermal heat pumps are 300% efficient: for every unit of electricity required for the pump, they provide 3 units of heat.

✅ The average UK home could save up to £300 a year on fuel by replacing an old gas boiler with a new A-rated condensing boiler with a programmer, room thermostat and thermostatic radiator controls.

✅ The average domestic solar water-heating system reduces CO_2 emissions by around 500kg (1,100lb) per year.

✅ Upgrading to a more efficient boiler in an average cold-climate house could cut CO_2 emissions by 1.5–2.5 tonnes (3,300–5,500lb) a year.

 In Western countries, central heating accounts for up to 60% of CO_2 emissions from homes.

✅ Replace your oil- or gas-fired boiler with a carbon-neutral biomass-powered boiler and save up to 7 tonnes (15,400lb) of CO_2 emissions per year.

Every degree C/F by which you turn down your thermostat will cut your heating bill by about 10% and shave 300kg (660lb) of CO_2 from the average home's emissions.

 At the beginning of the 1970s, the average temperature inside a house was 14°C (57°F). By the early 21st century, this had risen to almost 20°C (68°F).

Try lowering the temperature on your room thermostat by 1°C/2°F a week until you get down to 18°C (64°F), which should be a comfortable level for most people.

 Switching the heating off half an hour before bedtime should cut your heating bill by about 5% – and you probably won't notice any drop in temperature.

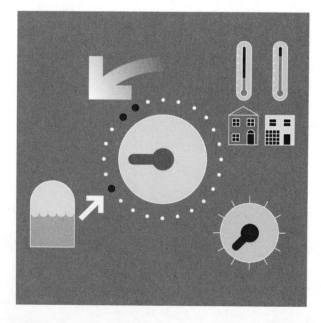

HEATING CONTROLS

Heating thermostats and controls are often tucked out of sight, but they can play a major role in reducing the amount of carbon your home generates.

LOCATE YOUR THERMOSTAT WISELY Make sure that it's on an internal wall in one of the main living areas in your home, so that it can accurately sense the ambient temperature. If it's too close to a heat source, such as an electric fire, television or lamp, it will overestimate the temperature. Conversely, if it's in a chilly utility room, it will underestimate the temperature, making your boiler work overtime.

HEAT AS YOU GO Heat only the rooms you're using, regulating each room separately with thermostatic radiator valves.

DON'T SCALD YOURSELF IN THE SHOWER Save energy by lowering your water-cylinder thermostat to 50–60°C (120–140°F). Any hotter than that and you'll only have to mix in cold water to make the temperature bearable.

BUTTONS AND DIALS

Used in a savvy way, the right kind of controls can cut your home heating costs by 15–20%. You'll need the following:

- a programmer, which allows you to set periods when your central heating and domestic hot water are on and off
- a room thermostat, which senses air temperature and switches the heating system on or off accordingly
- a cylinder thermostat (if you have a hot-water cylinder), which controls the temperature of your hot water supply
- thermostatic radiator valves, which sense the air temperature around them and switch the radiator off and on accordingly.
- For maximum efficiency, fit a programmable room thermostat. This combines the functions of a programmer and a thermostat, allowing you to select temperatures for different times.

RADIATORS

GET BEHIND YOUR RADS
To get the most out of your radiators' hard work, try fitting a reflective panel onto the wall behind each one (particularly if it's an exterior wall). This ensures that their heat is reflected back into the room instead of soaking into the wall. Specially designed radiator panels made from aluminium foil laminates or aluminized plastic films are cheap and easy to install, or you can make your own using a piece of cardboard covered in aluminium foil.

Fit shallow shelving about 5cm (2in) above your radiators to guide heat into the room.

Your central-heating system will almost certainly be generating a significant proportion of your home's carbon footprint. Make sure you're getting the most out of it by using your radiators effectively.

DON'T HIDE YOUR HEAT In order to create a current of warm air, radiators and other heaters need space around them, so don't tuck them behind sofas or curtains, or you'll end up with warm furnishings and cold rooms.

HONE YOUR TRV STRATEGY The only radiator on which you shouldn't fit a thermostatic valve (see p.27) is the one in the same room as your main thermostat. If this radiator already has a thermostatic valve, keep it on its highest setting so that your boiler doesn't end up overheating the rest of the house before your thermostat gets the message that things are hot enough.

BLEED YOUR RADIATORS REGULARLY to expel trapped air. This will help to keep them working at maximum efficiency.

Fitting reflective panels behind all your radiators could cut your home's CO_2 emissions by up to 200kg (440lb) a year.

 Moving a large piece of furniture away from a radiator could increase the radiator's efficiency by up to 20%.

⚠ Radiators near the top of multi-storey buildings may need to be bled more often than most, as hot air tends to rise through the heating system.

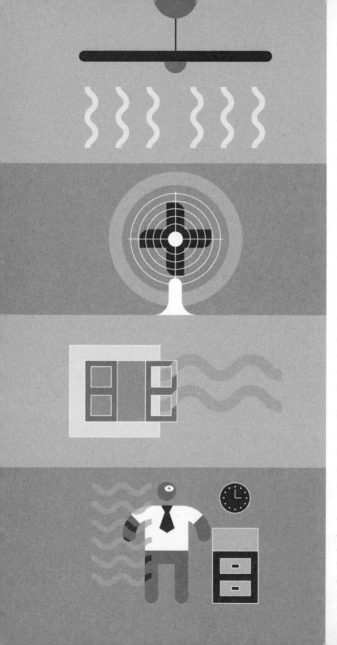

Replace your air-conditioning unit with a ceiling fan and you could cut your energy consumption from 1–2kW to the equivalent of a 100W lightbulb.

Using water from Lake Ontario to cool its downtown city buildings, the Canadian city of Toronto has reduced its annual CO_2 emissions by around 80,000 tonnes (88,000 US tons).

Regularly cleaning the filters in your home air-conditioning system can cut its energy use by 5%, reducing CO_2 emissions by 80–160kg (180–350lb) a year.

Houses that don't have air conditioning typically use about half as much energy as those that do.

Air conditioning uses up to a sixth of the electricity in the US, and on hot summer days consumes 43% of the US peak power load.

AIR CONDITIONING

Mechanical air chilling has a heavy environmental cost. As temperatures rise, low-carbon alternatives will be key to comfortable 21st-century living.

GO BACK TO BASICS Before installing any form of air-cooling system, improve your insulation (see pp.20–22) and draught-proofing (see pp.18–19) and look for ways to provide natural shading (see pp.16–17). These measures can often keep buildings cool without any need for mechanical intervention.

ENCOURAGE A NATURAL BREEZE Open windows in the evening to circulate cool air in and warm air out. Try running a large fan in the attic during the evening when the windows are open to pull cool air through the house.

DRESS FOR THE WEATHER Wear loose, cool clothing so you don't need air conditioning to counter the effects of too many layers. If necessary, ask your workplace to modify its dress code accordingly.

USE AIR CON CLEVERLY
If you do have air conditioning, work through this checklist to ensure that your system is as energy-efficient as it can be:

- make sure it's the right capacity for your home – it's a waste of energy to have too powerful a system
- seal its ducts to maximize efficiency
- clean or replace the filters regularly
- locate it well away from any heat-generating appliances, which could make it work harder than necessary
- keep windows and doors closed when it's running, or the cooled air will escape
- use it just to take the edge off the heat, rather than creating a polar microclimate
- turn it off about an hour before you go out – the air will still be cool by the time you're ready to leave.

LED IS BEST

Light-emitting diodes (LEDs) last five times longer than halogen bulbs and use 80% less energy to produce the same amount of light. By replacing all the bulbs in your home with LEDs, you could reduce your carbon dioxide emissions by up to 55kg (120lb) per year. This is equivalent to the emissions created by driving your car for roughly 300km (190 miles).

LIGHTING

A large proportion of the electricity we use is for lighting. Take advantage of natural sunlight and new technologies for brighter ways of lighting your home.

MAXIMIZE YOUR USE OF NATURAL LIGHT
For example, paint walls in light colours to brighten rooms, keep curtains and blinds open during the day to let in as much sunlight as possible, and make sure your windows are clean! If you work at home, situate your workspace in a naturally light room to minimize the need for artificial lighting.

SWITCH YOUR LIGHT When you do need to use electric lighting, avoid incandescent and halogen bulbs. Compact fluorescent lightbulbs (CFLs) were previously the most efficient bulbs but it is now best to choose light-emitting diodes (LEDs), which are more efficient and turn on instantly at full brightness.

IDENTIFY YOUR PRIORITIES It may not be feasible to replace all your bulbs at once, in which case prioritize the rooms that are lit for the longest periods. In 2021, the UK banned the sale of halogen bulbs. While many countries are phasing them out, shops may be allowed to sell old stock, so check carefully before buying.

Lighting makes up 15% of the average UK household electricity consumption.

Only 5% of the electricity used in old-style incandescent light bulbs converts into visible light.

The average LED lightbulb lasts for 15 to 20 years.

By switching to LED, the average UK household could save up to £7 per bulb per year.

In the UK, turning lights off when not needed could prevent up to 400,000 tonnes (440,000 US tons) of CO_2 emissions each year – that's almost 7kg (15lb) per person.

PIPE SUNLIGHT INTO YOUR HOME

You can take advantage of the sun's light by using suntubes or sunpipes – tubes with super-reflective interior surfaces – to direct light from outside into dimly lit areas within a building. They were first used 4,000 years ago by the Egyptians, who used light shafts and mirrors to bring daylight down into the centre of the Pyramids. Modern equivalents are simple and relatively inexpensive: sunlight falling on a plastic dome on an exterior wall or roof is intensified down the tube and then diffused through an opaque light fixture. Sunpipes can provide the equivalent of 100W of light in the winter and up to 500W on a sunny summer day.

  TURN LIGHTS OFF when you don't need them. If you're having a new house or extension built, make sure that light switches are located near the door to each room, to make it easier to switch off the lights when you leave the room.

 USE A TASK LAMP to focus light just where you need it, rather than lighting up an entire room.

 LOCATE LAMPS IN THE CORNERS of rooms, as they will reflect more light than if positioned more centrally along a wall.

 PUT NIGHT LIGHTS ON A TIMER if you must have them on at night, and make sure that your outdoor security lights have motion sensors so that they come on only when they need to.

ELECTRONIC APPLIANCES

Modern homes are packed full of electronic devices – from games consoles to tablets and TVs. They may be using more power than you realize.

($) **BE LABEL-CONSCIOUS** When you really need a new appliance, choose certified energy-efficient equipment. Look for the "Energy Saving Recommended" logo in the UK, the "Energy Star" logo in the US, or the Eco-label (a flower with blue stars circling a green E) in the EU.

($) **LOOK FOR INTEGRATED APPLIANCES** They have lower embodied energy (the energy embodied in their raw materials and manufacture) and use less energy to run than two separate pieces of kit.

($) **BUY AN INTELLIGENT CHARGER** – look for ones labelled "-dV". These reduce their energy use to a trickle once the appliance is charged, rather than continuing to suck up energy.

($) **USE CARBON-NEUTRAL GADGETS** Look for solar-powered or clockwork products such as radios and chargers. As technologies develop, more and more of these appliances are coming onto the market each year.

TIME TO PRESS THE "STOP" BUTTON

We have more gadgets in our homes than ever before. They account for a surprisingly large proportion of our domestic energy use – 19% of your total electric bill, with TVs being responsible for 30% of that usage. All these clever gizmos add up to a huge carbon impact – not just from the electricity they run off, but also from their manufacture and disposal.

We urgently need to buck this trend by:
• buying fewer appliances
• choosing more energy-efficient models
• using them more smartly
• avoiding regular upgrades
• repairing gadgets or going to a repair café
• buying reconditioned models
• shopping for products that are built to last, such as at buymeonce.com

KEEP TABS ON YOUR GADGETS

If you have trouble remembering to turn things off, a smart meter could help to remind you. Its digital display tells you exactly how much electricity your home's using at any given time, how much CO_2 is being emitted as a result, and how much is being added to your electricity bill. It has a wireless display unit, which means that it's easy to monitor. Studies suggest that smart meters can help households to cut their electricity use by up to 25% – and they're a great way of keeping an eye on the kids' gadget use or quickly checking that you haven't left the iron or grill on before you leave the house!

SWITCH OFF PROPERLY Televisions, videos and other electronic equipment can use nearly as much energy when left on standby as when they're in use. To avoid wasting energy, switch your equipment off at the mains when you're not using it. Make things as easy as possible: plug multiple devices into a power strip, which will enable you to switch them all off at once.

REDUCE THE BRIGHTNESS of your TV or device's screen. This can cut your power consumption by 30–50%. The factory setting is often much brighter than necessary. If you have an LCD TV, you can usually turn down the backlight.

BOX CLEVER If you need to buy a new TV, consider energy efficiency. Rear-projection TVs tend to be the most efficient, followed by LCD models. Cathode-ray tube and plasma TVs are generally the least energy-efficient.

Switching off appliances at the mains could cut your electricity bills by up to 10%.

A study in California found that the average household has 19 appliances on standby at any one time.

Go small screen – a TV with a 20-inch screen can use up to 10 times less electricity than one with a 50-inch screen.

In the US, more than 40,000kg (88,000lb) of CDs become obsolete each month. Download music to avoid adding to this waste.

Electronic appliances left in standby mode account for 8% of all domestic power consumption in the UK.

Use a wind-up radio, rather than a 20W model, for 4 hours a day and save about 12kg (26lb) of CO_2 a year.

Turning your Wi-Fi off at night can save £3 a year for the average UK household.

MOBILE PHONES AND TABLETS

Mobile phones and tablets are an ever more prominent part of modern life, and their contribution to energy demand is also growing at an alarming rate.

👍 **UNPLUG YOUR CHARGER** when it's not in use. Even if nothing's attached, many chargers still use energy (if it feels warm, it's using electricity). Don't charge your phone or device up to 100% – most have a longer lifespan if their batteries are kept around 50% charged.

💲 **RESIST THE LURE OF REGULAR UPGRADES** Companies are forever encouraging us to switch to the newest model – usually long before the existing one's defunct. Avoid this waste of raw materials (and the energy that goes into manufacture) by choosing a robust model that will last.

👍 **PASS YOUR OLD DEVICE ON** to charity for recycling when you really do need a new one. They contain a cocktail of toxic substances. Recycling keeps these undesirable elements out of the waste stream and saves the mining and manufacturing impacts of making new devices.

Unless it's a -dV charger (see p.35), a phone charger left plugged in all the time will waste up to 95% of the energy it consumes.

In the UK alone, 75,000 mobile phones are dropped into the toilet every year.

Mobile phone chargers can use up to 5W of electricity every hour when plugged in even without the phone attached.

In the UK, people replace their mobiles every 18 months on average; 15 million handsets are discarded each year; and only 5% of them are recycled.

The average mobile phone contains around 30 elements, including copper, lithium, lead and chromium, which can be toxic in combination in landfill.

Unplug your phone charger when it's not in use and avoid emitting up to 7kg (12lb) of CO_2 each year.

FUN IN THE SUN

For zero-emission cooking, try a solar oven, which allows you to bake, boil or steam food in about the same time it would take on a normal stove, using only the sun's energy. They're ideal for picnics or camping trips – particularly in areas where fires are prohibited – or you could set one up in your garden throughout the summer. For cooking on cloudy days or at night, hybrid versions with an energy-efficient electric back-up are available.

COOKERS

Cookers can vary greatly in their energy consumption, so when it's time to get a new one, it's well worth seeking out the most efficient model available.

 CHOOSE AN ELECTRIC COOKER These are now the more energy-efficient choice, especially if your electricity supply is renewable. Team this with an induction hob, which uses less energy and cooks quickly. Remember to check the product's energy efficiency label.

 LOOK FOR A CONVECTION (OR FAN) OVEN, which will enable you to cut cooking times by up to 30% and temperatures by around 20%.

 USE THE MAIN OVEN ONLY WHEN NECESSARY Cook small meals in a toaster oven, which will use less than half as much energy.

 GO MICRO Microwave ovens can greatly reduce energy consumption for certain types of cooking, especially heating small portions and leftovers. However, they're a very inefficient way of thawing frozen foods. Slow cookers are also very energy-efficient.

Cooking accounts for about 4% of domestic energy use for the average household.

Cook meals from scratch – food manufacturing is responsible for about three times as much carbon emission as home cooking.

The average UK family uses their stove hob about 400 times a year and their oven about 200 times a year.

A traditional Aga is one of the least energy-efficient ways to cook and can consume as much energy over a year as some people's entire home.

10,000 people microwaving one meal each instead of using an electric oven would save enough energy to heat a hot tub for a year.

Turn your microwave off at the mains when not in use. If not, the digital clock could use almost as much energy over the course of a year as the microwave itself.

The carbon footprint of a boiled potato is more dependent on whether you cook it with the lid on or off than how and where it was farmed.

A kettle or gas cooker generates about 1kg (2lb) of greenhouse gas for every 10 litres (2 gallons) of liquid boiled.

Placing a 15cm (6in) pan on a 20cm (8in) ring wastes 40% of the ring's energy.

Choosing the right size pan for cooking and keeping the lid on for most of the cooking process can reduce energy use by up to 90%.

Keep surfaces of cooking appliances clean and shiny to maximize the amount of heat that's reflected toward the food that you're cooking.

COOKING TECHNIQUES

Cooking food accounts for about 4% of the energy we use in our homes, so make sure your culinary skills aren't draining resources unnecessarily.

👍 **COOK IN BATCHES** If you're cooking from scratch, prepare enough for several meals, and freeze or refrigerate the remaining portions. It will take much less energy (and time and effort) to reheat the leftovers than to cook new meals.

👍 **USE THE SMALLEST PAN POSSIBLE**, as smaller pans require less energy.

👍 **MATCH THE PAN TO THE RING** If the pan doesn't completely cover the ring, heat will be escaping around the sides.

👍 **USE FLAT-BOTTOMED PANS** on electric elements to ensure maximum conduction.

👍 **WORK ON A NUMBER OF LEVELS** Cook several items on top of each other in a stacked steamer to get the most out of each ring's energy.

👍 **DON'T PREHEAT THE OVEN**, unless you're making pastry, bread or soufflé. It should get hot quickly enough not to affect cooking times or quality.

IT AIN'T WHAT YOU DO ...

While getting the kit right is important (see pp.40–41), it's actually the way that we cook food that has the bigger impact on energy use in the kitchen. A study by the United States Bureau of Standards has shown that some people use 50% less energy than others to cook the same meal.

TIME IS ENERGY

Not surprisingly, anything we can do to reduce cooking times will generally save energy. In the hurly-burly of preparing the evening meal after work, try to bear in mind some of the following straightforward time- and energy-saving techniques:

- keep pans covered while cooking
- chop food into small pieces
- defrost frozen food in the fridge overnight rather than cooking from frozen
- boil water for cooking in the kettle and then transfer it to the pan

- unless you're using the cooking water to make soup, use only enough water to cover the food you're boiling
- use a pressure cooker: by building up steam pressure, these cookers cook at a higher temperature, reducing cooking time and using 50–75% less energy than a normal saucepan.

A notable exception to the "time is energy" principle is the energy-saving technique of sit-boiling, which can be used for cooking rice, pasta and vegetables. As soon as the water is at a boil, put the food in the pan, cover with a tight-fitting lid and turn the heat off completely. The food will cook in the residual heat, but will take around 50% longer than usual.

A pop-up toaster uses up to three times less energy than the grill in your oven.

SAY GOODBYE TO READY MEALS When time's tight and you're tempted to reach for an oven-ready meal, why not whip up a stir-fry instead? It will take a quarter of the time and energy to cook – and that's not including the energy involved in the production of the ready meal.

LET IT BE Resist the temptation to open the oven door to check progress. Every time you do so, up to 25% of the heat escapes.

TURN OFF THE HEAT a few minutes before food's cooked – it'll continue cooking in the residual heat. Then, after you've taken your meal out, supplement your central heating by leaving the oven door open.

ALL UNDER ONE LID Cook whole meals in one pot. Delicious one-pot paellas, minestrones, dhals and casseroles use about a third of the energy of meals cooked in separate pans.

COMPLEAT YOUR VEG Compleating means eating all edible parts of fruits and vegetables. This creative cooking technique reduces your kitchen's waste and saves money. Try dishes such as carrot top pesto, veggie peel crisps, onion skin stock or apple core cider vinegar. For more waste-free recipes like this and lots more compleating tips and tricks, check out my other book, *The Complete Book of Vegan Compleating*!

REFRIGERATION

Humming away 24/7, fridges and freezers account for about a quarter of domestic electricity consumption. So make sure they're not costing you or the environment more than necessary by using them as efficiently as possible.

LOCATION IS EVERYTHING Install your fridge or freezer in a cool spot, well away from your cooker, boiler and radiators, with a gap of at least 6cm (2in) for air to circulate behind it. Placing your appliance in a cool setting could cut associated CO_2 emissions by up to 150kg (330lb) per year.

SPRING CLEAN Keep the coils at the back of your fridge or freezer dust-free. This will improve its efficiency by up to 30%.

CHECK YOUR TEMPERATURE Fridges don't need to be any cooler than 3–5°C (about 40°F), and freezers do their job at –15°C (5°F). Any colder and they're wasting energy and your money. Invest in a fridge/freezer thermometer if there isn't one built in.

DEFROST REGULARLY (when the ice is 3–5mm (1/10–1/5in) thick) or choose a frost-free model. A frosted-up freezer uses more energy.

CHILLING WITHOUT ELECTRICITY

Downsize your chilling by using a small fridge only for things that need to be kept really cold, and a naturally cool cupboard or larder (with an airbrick installed in an external wall if you live in a reasonably cool climate) for the rest of your food.

FOOD FOR THOUGHT

You can take some of the burden off your fridge and freezer by being aware of the effects of the items you put in them. Here are some strategies to help you maximize efficiency:

- Wait for food to cool before you put it in the fridge, and make sure it's covered (ideally with a lid or plate rather than foil or cling film). This not only stops your food drying out, but stops the moisture it contains condensing on the fridge/freezer walls, which makes the appliance use more energy and need defrosting more often.

- Plan ahead so you don't need to use your cooker or microwave to defrost frozen food. If you can let frozen food thaw in the fridge overnight, its chilliness will leave less work for the fridge to do.
- Keep your fridge three-quarters full and freezer completely full for optimum efficiency. This ensures that when you open the fridge there's less air to escape. Use newspaper to fill the freezer and keep water-filled bottles in the fridge if you haven't got enough food to maintain the appropriate capacity.

CHECK THE FRIDGE DOOR SEAL by putting a piece of paper in it. If the paper slips out when the door's closed, you may need to change the seal and/or door magnets to stop cool air escaping.

KEEP YOUR FRIDGE TIDY to help you find what you're looking for quickly. Up to 30% of the cool air held within the fridge escapes every time you open the door, so the quicker you can grab stuff and close the door, the better.

VACATION PREPARATION Before you go away, make sure your fridge is as empty as possible. If there are things that will last until you get back, turn the power down to chill these few items. Otherwise turn the fridge off completely.

TAKE IT OUT OF CIRCULATION Normally, passing on items you no longer want to people who can make use of them is a great way to save energy associated with the production of new goods. However, this principle doesn't apply to energy-guzzling old fridges and freezers. When you're replacing a decrepit fridge or freezer, don't put it on the second-hand market, but send it to be dismantled by an approved recycler.

SHARING IS CARING Community fridges and food-sharing schemes and apps are increasingly popular as a way to swap, share and collect excess or unwanted food that might otherwise have gone to landfill. Your glut of courgettes could be just what someone is looking for!

Nearly 20% of the energy generated worldwide is used for refrigeration.

 The most efficient fridge-freezers are those with the freezer above or below the fridge. They use 10–25% less energy than side-by-side models.

 Unplugging an underused spare freezer can cut a home's CO_2 emissions by about 10%.

Manual-defrost freezers use much less energy than auto-defrost models (as long as you defrost them regularly!).

Features such as ice makers and through-the-door water dispensers can increase a fridge-freezer's energy use by up to 20%.

New, energy-efficient models can use a third of the energy of a 10-year-old appliance.

⚠ One million plastic bottles are used by the world's population every minute.

✓ UK pubs throw away 600,000 tonnes (660,000 US tons) of glass bottles every year – so drink draught beer to avoid contributing to this waste.

⚠ For every 15 litres (3 gallons) of bottled water transported to the UK from France, a litre (⅕ gallon) of diesel is used.

✓ Importing wine in bulk and bottling it at its destination rather than at source can reduce its carbon footprint by up to 40%.

⚠ Keep your water-boiling as brief as possible: switching on a typical 2,400W kettle is the equivalent of switching on 160 energy-saving lightbulbs at once.

✓ Carry a refillable water bottle and use the Refill app to find businesses which are happy to refill your bottle for free. The app also lists spots for coffee cup refills, bring-your-own-container takeaway meals and zero-waste shopping.

⚠ Bottled water costs up to 10,000 times as much as tap water.

✓ Using a mug at work twice a day rather than disposable cups will avoid emitting around 60kg (130lb) of CO_2 a year.

DRINKS

Whatever your tipple, make sure it's not racking you up an excessive carbon footprint along with your bar bill.

👍 **BOIL ONLY AS MUCH WATER AS YOU NEED**
Completely filling the kettle just for one cup of tea releases an unnecessary 125 cups of CO_2. To take out the guesswork, use a mug to pour in the required number of measures.

💲 **BUY SHADE-GROWN COFFEE**, which helps preserve ecosystems that sequester some of the CO_2 produced in making your daily brew.

💲 **DRINK A LOCALLY BREWED PINT** and you'll enjoy an ale of high quality and individuality that also has low "beer mileage".

💲 **TRY ORGANIC WINES**, from as close to home as possible. You'll avoid the use of gallons of petroleum distillates and hundreds of pounds of petroleum-derived pesticides as well as cutting the wine miles needed to shift this heavy treat.

CAP YOUR BOTTLED WATER CONSUMPTION
Chilled tap water tastes almost exactly the same as bottled mineral water, costs a tiny fraction of the price, and is delivered, packaging-free, by pipe, not truck. Keep a jug of it in the fridge. If you're worried about water quality, invest in a filtration system for your kitchen and have purified water literally on tap. To avoid having to buy bottled water when you're out and about, pack a small, robust drinking bottle and refill it en route.

Grow your own chamomile, lemon balm or mint for herbal tea rather than always using factory-made tea bags.

Studies suggest that using a dishwasher can be more energy-efficient than washing dishes by hand. However, the energy- (and carbon-) saving benefits depend entirely on good technique. If you use a dishwasher:

- run it only when there's a full load – or, if you're desperate, use the half-load economy cycle
- use as low a temperature as possible
- don't pre-rinse items unless they're covered with burnt-on or dried-on food
- regularly clean the filter
- dry your dishes naturally by opening the dishwasher before it begins the drying cycle; the hot dishes will dry quickly on their own
- turn it off when it's not in use – leaving the dishwasher on when it's not running can consume 70% as much power as it uses during the actual wash cycle.

DOING THE DISHES

Washing the dishes can be a tedious chore. Keep it quick, energy- and water-efficient and carbon-light by getting into good habits at the sink or dishwasher.

HAND-WASH CAREFULLY If done right, doing the dishes by hand will almost certainly be more energy-efficient than using a dishwasher – especially for small volumes of dishes. Rather than washing them under a running tap, put a plug in the sink, or use a washing-up bowl. And to minimize the amount of water you use when rinsing, install a low-flow aerator on your kitchen sink taps.

SOAK FOOD-ENCRUSTED PANS IN SOAPY WATER before you wash them up or put them in the dishwasher – that way, you'll use less water and energy overall to get them clean.

CHOOSE A WATER- AND ENERGY-EFFICIENT DISHWASHER that's the right size for your lifestyle. Look for one with a soil-sensor, which adjusts water and energy use depending on how dirty the dishes are in each load.

A certified energy-saving dishwasher uses up to 40% less energy than most older models, cutting carbon emissions by about 70kg (150lb) a year.

Running your dishwasher on an economy setting and halving the number of times you use it could cut your CO_2 emissions by over 100kg (220lb) a year.

Collect old "grey" washing-up water in a bowl and use it to flush the toilet or water plants, rather than sending it down the drain.

When washing dishes by hand, minimize the number of times you need to change the water by washing the least-dirty items first.

A 55°C (130°F) dishwasher cycle uses about a third less energy than a 65°C (150°F) cycle.

Avoid aerosol sprays – they contain a high proportion of packaging to contents and are difficult to recycle.

✅ Tree-lined streets have up to two-thirds fewer dust particles in the air than streets without any form of vegetation.

✅ Dirt is good for you! Studies suggest that children who grow up in too clean an environment may be more susceptible to allergies and asthma.

✅ Use white vinegar to clean taps, windows, floors, tiles, etc., rather than buying a range of specialized products.

✅ Buy cleaning products in bulk or from a refill shop and decant them into reusable containers.

CLEANING PRODUCTS

The simple act of cleaning our homes has become an energy-intensive, product-laden process that can have an unnecessarily large environmental impact.

KEEP DIRT OUT Try planting trees or a hedge between your home and the road – the vegetation will capture a lot of dust before it reaches your home.

USE REUSABLE SCRUBBERS AND CLOTHS OR RAGS instead of paper towels or disposable wipes. Avoid cleaning materials made of plastic, which shed harmful microplastics as you clean. Instead choose reusables made of bamboo, organic cotton or coconut fibres.

CHOOSE PRODUCTS THAT WORK WELL AT LOW TEMPERATURES, such as floor cleaner that performs well with cold rather than hot water, or make your own.

OPT FOR CONCENTRATED PRODUCTS to minimize the impacts of processing, transporting and packaging your cleaning materials.

NATURE ABHORS A VACUUM!

The average vacuum cleaner uses ten times more electricity per hour than a computer – most of the energy is converted into heat rather than suction. Be smart with your vacuum cleaner to minimize its carbon footprint:

- when choosing a new vacuum cleaner, look for the most energy-efficient model and choose a bagless one
- reduce the need to clean your floors by placing doormats on each side of external doors and take your shoes off when you come in
- use a broom, dustpan and brush, or carpet sweeper as a carbon-free alternative.

TOILET TACTICS

The process of collecting, purifying and distributing tap water has a significant carbon footprint – about 0.3kg (^{2}/$_3$lb) of CO_2 for every 1,000 litres (220 gallons) of water. Yet we use it as though it were in limitless supply. For example, up to a third of the drinking water that comes into the average Western home goes straight down the toilet, which is a ridiculous waste of this precious resource. To stem the flow, try putting some of these flushing tips into action:

- Put a plastic bottle filled with water into the cistern to reduce the volume per flush. Or use a product, such as the "Hippo" or "Save-a-Flush", that has been specially designed to do the same job.
- If you're installing a new toilet, specify one that uses low flush volumes or allows you to choose flush volume according to "load".

PERSONAL HYGIENE & GROOMING

Whether your bathroom is a luxurious retreat or a morning battleground, it's likely that your household's bathing habits have a significant carbon footprint, which can be easily trimmed without leaving you grubby.

👍 **SWITCH FROM A DAILY BATH TO A SHOWER** The average bath contains about 80 litres (17½ gallons) of water, while a five-minute shower uses around 30 litres (6½ gallons). Save baths for special occasions – pour yourself a glass of (organic) wine, add a few drops of natural bath oil and put on some soothing music. And if you're in a position to do so, save water by sharing your bath …

👍 **KEEP YOUR SHOWERS SHORT** If you spend much longer than five minutes in the shower you'll soon find you're using as much water as you would in the bath. Use a shower timer to remind you when your time's up.

💲 **AVOID POWER SHOWERS**, which can pump out 15 litres (3 gallons) of hot water a minute, so a five-minute shower will use just as much water as a bath.

The average person would save about 550,000 litres (120,000 gallons) of water over a lifetime by switching off the tap while brushing their teeth.

Saving just 20 litres (4 gallons) of hot water per day will cut your energy usage by up to 700kWh per year, cutting CO_2 emissions by 140kg (310lb).

⚠
Only 50% of bathroom waste gets recycled, such as shampoo bottles, toothpaste tubes and toilet paper rolls – that's compared to 90% of waste in the kitchen.

✓
Putting a "Hippo" in your toilet cistern saves up to 5,000 litres (1,100 gallons) of water and avoids the emission of about 1.5kg (3lb) of CO_2 per year.

⚠
Water heating accounts for around a quarter of the average home's energy usage.

⚠
In the US, around 2 billion disposable razors are sent to landfill every year.

- Think about whether you really need to flush every time you use the toilet.
- To avoid all the environmental (and financial) costs of using processed drinking water for flushing, connect your toilet(s) to a rainwater harvesting unit or a system that recycles "grey" water (water that's been used in sinks, baths, showers or the washing machine). Rainwater and "grey" water are of perfectly adequate quality for flushing the toilet. For a quick fix, have a bucket of old "grey" washing-up or shower water next to your toilet. Pour this into the loo to flush away anything yellow!
- You could also investigate toilets that separate the different kinds of waste going into them, reducing the energy needed to convert "yellow", "grey" and "black" water into drinking-quality water.

 INSTALL LOW-FLOW AERATING FITTINGS to your shower and taps. These halve the flow and mix air bubbles into the water, which makes you feel that you're getting just as wet. A family of four can cut their CO_2 emissions by over 200kg (440lb) a year by switching from a normal shower to a low-flow shower head.

 TURN OFF THE TAP while you brush your teeth and you'll save up to 10 litres (2 gallons) of water each time you brush your teeth.

TAKE THE HEAT OFF YOUR HAIR Save yourself time in the morning and cut your beauty regime's carbon footprint by having a low-maintenance haircut that doesn't need blitzing with a blow-dry and straighteners every day.

 SHAVE AWAY YOUR CARBON FOOTPRINT Extend the life of your razor blades with a razor cartridge sharpener, which could cut down your razor consumption by up to 75%. Or move away from disposable blades: buy a rechargeable electric shaver, reusable safety razor or get to grips with a cut-throat razor. If looked after properly, it will give you a lifetime of smooth shaves.

STOP THE
TIDE OF PLASTIC

Avoid creating plastic waste
from your bathroom by shopping smart:

Refill reusable bottles at a zero-waste shop, for
liquids such as shower gel or toilet cleaner.

Switch to a shampoo bar to replace your
bottled shampoo and conditioner.

Replace your shower gel and liquid hand soap with a bar of soap.

Try natural deodorant, sold in a recyclable aluminium tin or jar.

Choose plastic-free oral care, such as natural floss,
toothpaste tablets and toothpowder.

Switch to natural menstrual products, such as period pants,
a menstrual cup and plastic-free tampons or pads.

Choose plastic-free and compostable cotton buds (cotton swabs).

Buy recycled or bamboo toilet paper.

Replace throwaway wet wipes with reusable
facial rounds or a flannel.

The average UK washing machine is used 274 times a year.

 Using a washing line instead of a tumble dryer could avoid 600–650kg (1,300–1,400lb) of CO_2 emissions a year.

 In the US, around 1,100 loads of washing are started every second.

LAUNDRY

Washing machines and tumble dryers certainly take the hard work out of doing the laundry, but they involve a lot of heating, so their carbon cost is high. Use them wisely and your conscience will be as clean as your clothes.

($) **INVEST IN AN ENERGY-SAVING MACHINE**, which could cut your washing's energy consumption by up to a third. Look for a machine with a high spin speed. This will remove most of the water from your clothes, reducing the need for tumble drying.

($) **GO FROM TOP TO FRONT** If your current washing machine is a top-loader, buy a front-loading model when you need a replacement. Although top-loaders tend to have a greater capacity, front-loaders use a fraction of the water and energy, and treat clothes more gently.

👍 **PRESOAK PARTICULARLY GRUBBY CLOTHES** before putting them in the washing machine to avoid the need for a hot wash and large amounts of detergent.

👍 **WASH FEWER LOADS** Cutting down by just one wash per week can avoid 20–30kg (45–55lb) of CO_2 emissions each year. Wait until clothes are actually dirty before you wash them (hanging them up to air between wearings will help to

PRESSING MATTERS
Save time and energy by ironing only what you really need to. Ironing in large batches using a spray bottle filled with water instead of the steam setting will significantly cut your iron's energy use. And save the clothes that require a cooler iron until last. That way you can turn the iron off before you get to them and press them flat with the residual heat.

The average US household washes around 6,000 items a year.

WASHING ALL OVER THE WORLD

Up to 90% of the energy used for washing clothes goes into heating the water, so the temperature of your wash makes a huge difference to its carbon footprint.

Worldwide, people have very different washing habits. In Spain, 85% of laundry loads are washed at temperatures below 40°C (104°F), compared to just 4% in the UK, where the average wash temperature, 43°C (109°F), is around twice as hot as that in Japan and twice as many loads are put on each week than in Germany. And in the US, the average laundry temperature is just 29°C (84°F), which is 13°C (55°F) cooler than the European average.

keep them fresh) and then wait until you've got a full load to avoid wasting water and energy.

WASH AT LOWER TEMPERATURES Washing clothes at 30°C (86°F) instead of a higher temperature uses up to 40% less energy, and your clothes will last longer. Seek out detergents designed to perform well at lower temperatures. This could cut your emissions by more than 200kg (440lb) a year.

CHOOSE KINDER CLEANERS Refill your liquid laundry products at a zero-waste shop in a reusable bottle, or try an alternative washing product such as the Ecoegg or soap nuts.

DRY WISELY When in operation, tumble dryers use more energy than almost any other household appliance, generating more than 3kg (6lb) of greenhouse gas for each load they dry. So, while they're obviously convenient, they should be used only as a last resort. Hang clothes out to dry instead (outside, if possible – this makes them smell really fresh). If you must use a tumble dryer, run loads back to back while the drum's still warm, and keep the lint collector and vent clear for optimum efficiency.

TRAP WASTE FIBRES When washed, our clothes shed microfibres which enter waterways and add to microplastic pollution. Avoid this unwanted waste by washing your clothes inside a washing bag, such as a Guppyfriend. The trapped microfibres can then be disposed of in a bin, and the bag can be reused again and again.

The UK wastes £170 million worth of energy a year by washing clothes at a higher temperature than necessary.

If everyone in the UK washed at 30°C (86°F), each year they'd save enough energy to power the country's streetlamps for 10 months.

A tumble dryer with a blocked-up lint collector or vent can use up to 30% more energy than a well-maintained one.

Avoiding the pre-wash setting cuts each load's energy use by up to 15%.

Calling all absent-minded ironers! If you need to buy a new iron, get one that switches itself off if left undisturbed for 10–15 minutes.

A dripping tap can waste more than 5,500 litres (1,200 gallons) of water a year.

Leaving a sprinkler on for an hour can consume the same amount of water as a family of four uses in two days.

The average household in the UK uses 345 litres (over 75 gallons) of water every day – that's 145 litres (over 30 gallons) per person per day.

Up to 80% of current UK water demand could be met if water that fell on roofs was captured.

WATER USE

We're using more water per person every year, and processing it requires huge amounts of energy, generating significant carbon emissions.

HARVEST THE RAIN Capture some of the rain that falls on your roof by connecting a water butt to a downpipe. This water can then be used in the garden. Many plants, such as blueberries, actually prefer to be watered with rain water. To take things further, consider installing a rain water harvesting system, which collects and filters rain water for use in your toilet and washing machine.

USE WATER TWICE with a WaterGreen™ – a simple hose with a small handpump that siphons water out of the bath for a second use in the garden or for flushing the loo.

WASH YOUR CAR WITH RAIN WATER If you can't use rain water, hand wash it using a bucket of water and a sponge or rag. If you really need to use a hose, fit it with a trigger, so you can turn it off between rinsings. This can save up to 700 litres (150 gallons) of water each time.

IRRIGATION INFORMATION

The type of plants that we put in our gardens and the way that we look after them can have a major bearing on the amount of water we use. Follow these water-saving irrigation tips and your garden will thrive in all weathers:

- plant drought-resistant species – Mediterranean plants such as rosemary, lavender, salvias and sage are very tolerant of long dry periods
- water in the early morning or evening to minimize evaporation
- use a watering can rather than a sprinkler and aim water at the base of your plants
- keep grass long (at least 4cm (1½in)) to shade the soil and stop it drying out
- mulch around your plants to help stop water from evaporating from the soil's surface, inhibit weed growth and add nutrients.

BACKYARD

Gardening, done the right way, can reduce your carbon footprint.

 RAKE UP DEAD LEAVES instead of using a leaf blower. Why not allow the leaves to naturally break down into the soil? Or make your own leafmould to add goodness to the soil.

MOW THE GREEN WAY Rather than using a petrol mower, go for an electric model (ideally powered by electricity from a green tariff) – or, even better, a manual one. Consider not mowing at all or less, especially during "No Mow May". Or give up your grass completely – lawns are a monoculture so why not replace yours with a nature-friendly wildflower patch or hedgerow?

PLANT TREES A tree can absorb more than a tonne (2,200lb) of CO_2 over its life. When it dies and decays, much of this is released back into the atmosphere (although a little is retained in the soil) – so ideally the tree should be used as timber when it dies, and another planted in its place. A small Acer is perfect for limited space, or an apple or cherry tree so you and wildlife can also enjoy its fruits.

AVOID LIGHTING BONFIRES Compost your garden waste instead (see pp.66–7).

Peat bogs are a vital carbon sink and a rare habitat. Help conserve this important environment by choosing peat-free compost or making your own.

In the US each year, as much petrol is spilled when filling lawn mowers as in the 1989 Exxon Valdez tanker disaster.

 Plant some bamboo, as it generates 35% more oxygen than an equivalent area of trees and also stores more CO_2.

Used for just two hours, the average patio heater produces as much CO_2 as a car does in an average day.

 The world's trees absorb around 26 million tonnes (28.5 million US tons) of CO_2 a year.

Using a petrol lawn mower for one hour creates the equivalent emissions of driving 160km (100 miles) in a car.

 Leave some areas wild and "imperfect" to help support micro- and macro-organisms and wildlife like hedgehogs and birds.

 Over 200 species of wildflowers have been found in UK lawns, and 80% of lawns support the equivalent of 400 bees a day! Make your lawn more biodiverse by mowing no more than once every four weeks and leaving some areas unmown.

In Dhaka, Bangladesh, all organic waste is composted, reducing methane emissions by 1,270 tonnes (1,400 US tons) a year, generating jobs and cleaning up the city – a model which is being replicated around the world.

25–30% of all food produced in the world is wasted, 70% of which is edible. Food waste is responsible for 8–10% of total man-made greenhouse gas emissions – roughly the same as the global aviation industry!

If food waste was removed from landfill, the level of greenhouse gas reduction would be equivalent to removing a fifth of all cars from UK roads.

Every year the UK produces enough garden waste to fill the Royal Albert Hall more than 70 times.

Composting your organic waste could cut CO_2 emissions by up to 300kg (660lb) a year, equivalent to around 1,200 – 1,600km (750–1,000 miles) of car travel.

Around 60% of the average UK household's refuse consists of biodegradable food, garden and paper waste.

Composting worms eat at least half their body weight in organic matter every day.

COMPOST

In a landfill, organic waste decomposes without oxygen, which causes it to give off methane, a potent greenhouse gas with 21 times the impact of CO_2. Composting averts this problem and creates natural fertilizer and soil conditioner.

MAKE YOUR OWN COMPOST Buy a simple composting bin or make your own: a timber frame can be made from recycled pallets and a lid added to keep out rain and retain heat.

EQUIP YOUR KITCHEN WITH A BOKASHI BUCKET This ingenious Japanese composter will deal with almost any kind of waste food (including cooked food, meat, fish and dairy) and is small enough to fit in the kitchen. It takes only a few weeks to break down your organic waste into soil improver for your garden and liquid fertilizer for your plants.

SET UP A WORMERY, a self-contained composting unit containing special species of worms which convert organic matter into vermicompost – a superb natural soil conditioner and plant food.

HEAPS OF ADVICE

For the best composting results:

- add roughly equal amounts of nitrogen-rich "green" matter, such as plants, leaves and vegetables, and carbon-rich "brown" matter, such as cardboard, paper and twigs
- you can also compost sawdust, eggshells, plastic-free teabags, coffee grounds and plastic-free filter papers, hair and farm manure
- don't compost big branches, painted wood, sawdust from plywood, coloured or coated paper, meat, fish, dairy products, diseased plants, waste and litter from carnivorous pets, or packaging marked as non-compostable
- turn the compost every few weeks to make sure it rots down properly
- make a dead hedge from old branches – a great way to slowly compost these while providing a habitat for nature.

Look for an allotment area or community garden in your neighbourhood. With a few hours' attention each week, a little patch of land could change the way your whole family eats.

If there aren't any plots available – or if you'd prefer not to be in sole charge of your crops – look for a Community Supported Agriculture (CSA) scheme in your area. These enable you to become involved in a local farm in return for a share of the harvest. Your involvement can take the form of a financial investment or time spent working on the farm – or you can simply buy your food directly from the farm through a box scheme (see p.78).

GROWING YOUR OWN

As well as buying local, seasonal, organic food, try growing your own for less food miles and packaging.

 GROW ORGANICALLY, (or veganically), avoiding chemical fertilizers and pesticides – and the greenhouse gases released in their production. Also try forest gardening or companion planting to naturally manage pests on your plot.

 A GOOD CUPPA Try making your own natural fertiliser with just water, stinging nettles and comfrey: leave to brew for a few weeks and then strain and dilute – this is known as tea.

 START A MICRO-GARDEN Grow herbs, salad or microgreens on your kitchen windowsill.

PLANT SOME FRUIT TREES Get free fruit, and the trees will absorb CO_2 as they grow.

 GROW YOUR OWN FLOWERS Avoid the CO_2 emissions associated with flowers grown in hothouses or flown vast distances. Plant bulbs, take cuttings of long-lasting shrubs or plant patches of native wildflowers.

GROW UP! Try vertical gardening: produce is grown in containers, or on a living wall, making the best of a little garden or balcony.

✅ Home-grown produce can be eaten minutes after being picked – when it's at its most nutritious.

✅ Reuse old plastic plant pots and choose plastic-free compostable planters when buying new. Old toilet paper rolls are ideal for upcycling as pots for growing seedlings.

✅ During World War II, "victory gardens" planted across the US supplied up to 40% of all vegetables consumed by American civilians.

⚠️ Tending lawns in the US uses around 1.2 trillion litres (260 billion gallons) of water a week – enough to water 30 million hectares (74 million acres) of organic vegetables all summer.

✅ A single apple tree can produce up to 500 apples per season for 20 years.

⚠️ Europe and the US are the biggest buyers of cut flowers, with the blooms arriving in refrigerated transport from as far as Kenya. In the UK, 90% of cut flowers are imported.

✅ Make mini-greenhouses, or cloches, for your seedlings by cutting the base off plastic bottles.

✅ Take cuttings and try seed saving, rather than buying new plants and seeds, to cut back on transport, avoid building up a mountain of plastic pots, and save money.

Make an art of salvaging – a great way to save money, keep valuable materials out of landfill and give your building project a unique character.

 A school in Sheffield, UK has been super-insulated – far beyond any official regulations – with 4,000 pairs of recycled jeans.

A concrete alternative called Hemcrete® actually absorbs carbon – locking in 110kg (240lb) of CO_2 per cubic metre.

 Producing 1 tonne (2,200lb) of cement releases around 700kg (1,500lb) of CO_2 into the atmosphere. Cement production accounts for about 5% of man-made CO_2 emissions.

 On average, using a cubic metre (35 cubic feet) of wood generates 800kg (1,760lb) less CO_2 than using the same volume of other building materials.

 Concrete can't be penetrated by rainwater and can increase the build-up of surface water by 50%, contributing to flash flooding. Instead, choose shingle, pebbles, grass or paving with permeable edges for paths, driveways and outdoor socializing areas.

BUILDING MATERIALS

Whether you're doing a spot of DIY or commissioning a dream home, try to minimize the energy that goes into making your building (its "embodied energy") and use building materials with a low carbon footprint.

($) **WOOD FOR GOOD** Substitute wood for other building materials where you can. Not only do trees absorb CO_2, but, in its processing, wood has the lowest energy consumption and the lowest CO_2 emissions of any common building material. It's also a great insulator. Make sure to use reclaimed or sustainably produced timber.

($) **AVOID CEMENT** – one of the most energy-intensive products in the world. If you need to use cement or concrete, try Hemcrete® – a highly insulating, low-carbon alternative made from lime and hemp.

SHARE AND SWAP Find or set up a local tool library to share things like power or gardening tools. Building materials can often be sourced from local community groups and places like Freecycle, leftover from other people's building projects.

GREEN YOUR ROOF
More and more people are creating "green roofs" by planting their roofs with vegetation. They provide excellent insulation. The plants absorb solar radiation, which stops it from entering the building – this is particularly desirable in cities, where the "heat island" effect can raise the local temperature by up to 10%. Green roofs also reduce storm-water run-off and provide habitats for a broad range of plants and creatures. If a green roof on your house isn't feasible, consider one for your shed, bike storage or garden shelters.

Does your local government have a green homes scheme or grant to help fund improvements to reduce your home's carbon impact?

DEMAND BETTER

Getting your head around ethical finances can feel overwhelming. Try to make one switch at a time. If that's not possible, write to or speak to your employer or service provider with your concerns and ask that they make improvements.

HOME IS WHERE THE HEART IS

Try to choose a responsible mortgage provider. Just like your pension and banking, check what your mortgage provider invests in. Some lenders now also offer incentives and schemes for greener properties based on your home's energy efficiency and environmental measures.

FINANCE

Would you choose to invest your money in industries such as fossil fuels, tobacco, arms and deforestation? Now might be the time to check what you are really funding and whether that aligns with your values.

($) **EVERY PENNY COUNTS** Your current account, savings or investment fund could have a positive or negative impact on people and the planet. Look for businesses that are transparent about what your money will finance. Does it invest in renewable energy or fossil fuels, for example? Also consider whether it pays employees a fair wage and runs its business and offices in a low-waste and ethical manner.

($) **INVEST IN THE FUTURE** The majority of pension companies invest your money by backing industries that can include fossil fuels and deforestation. However, some pensions fund green projects such as renewable energy, cleaner transport and reforestation. Typically, your employer enrols you in a default pension. Speak to your pension provider and find out which fund your money is in and what it finances. Enquire about alternative funds, consider moving to a green provider and use Good With Money's online Good Guide to Pensions (www.good-with-money.com) to compare.

Having a sustainable pension can reduce your carbon footprint 27 times more than giving up flying and becoming a vegan combined.

Of all the money invested in the UK, around half comes from our pension savings.

 68% of UK savers want their investments to consider people and planet alongside profit.

We've got used to eating what we want whenever we want it, ignoring the fact that transporting out-of-season food vast distances has a huge environmental impact. The benefits of buying local, seasonal food are varied and considerable:

- it cuts back on the environmental impacts of transportation
- it generally requires less energy-hungry packaging, processing and refrigeration
- it's fresher, tastier and more nutritious (long-distance produce is often picked before it has ripened to help it survive the lengthy journey)
- more varieties are available – not just the ones that can withstand long trips
- it supports small local growers and brings money into your local economy.

EATING LOCAL

The food you've eaten today may well have travelled thousands of miles to your plate, clocking up significant carbon emissions en route. Cut back on your "carbs" each meal by choosing locally produced, seasonal food whenever you can.

GROW YOUR OWN FOOD and trim food miles down to food metres (see pp.68–9).

STREET PLAN When it's time to plant seeds, coordinate with like-minded neighbours so that you don't all grow the same crops and can share a range of produce, rather than having a glut of one or two. You might even be lucky enough to have a local seed-sharing scheme or swap point.

BECOME A "LOCAVORE" There is a movement of people, known as "locavores", who restrict their diet to foods sourced within a certain range – for example, a radius of 160km (100 miles). Why not try joining them? If you find this ruling too strict, don't be afraid to allow yourself occasional treats, such as tropical fruit, from further afield, and apply this rule primarily to everyday foodstuffs. You could even try foraging local wild food, such as blackberries and wild garlic.

SHOP LOCALLY Make sure you're not adding to your groceries' carbon footprint by making unnecessary car journeys to out-of-town shopping centres: minimize car trips and shop close to home.

BUY IN SEASON and enjoy a constantly changing parade of produce that's locally produced and at its prime throughout the year. Eating local and seasonal could cut your carbon footprint by as much as 600–700kg (1,300-1,500lb) a year.

CELEBRATE SEASONAL FOOD by attending local food fairs and festivals.

GET INTO A PICKLE To enjoy your favourite foods all year round without flying them in from the other side of the world when they're out of season, buy them in bulk when they are in season and make delicious pickles, chutneys and jams with them.

SPREAD THE WORD Invite your friends to a locally sourced dinner to show them how well you can eat using just local, seasonal ingredients.

GREENHOUSE EFFECT
Locally grown produce doesn't always have a lower carbon footprint than the same food grown thousands of miles away. The pressure to supply fruit and vegetables out of their normal season is persuading some farmers in cold-climate countries to grow crops such as tomatoes and salads in heated greenhouses year-round. This can use as much if not more energy than transporting them from sunnier climes. However, the controlled environment of these hydroponic greenhouses does reduce the need for pesticides. For tastier, lower carbon produce, try to enjoy it seasonally when nature intended.

⚠ The meat industry generates 18% of the world's greenhouse gas emissions – that's more than from all forms of transport.

 ⚠ Producing 1kg (2lb) of meat is responsible for more greenhouse emissions than going for a 3-hour drive while leaving all the lights on at home.

 ✓ Avoiding meat and dairy is one of the single biggest things an individual can do to reduce their carbon footprint.

⚠ 30–40% of UK fish stocks are overfished. What's more, discarded fishing nets and waste are the biggest contributor to ocean plastic, making up a shocking 46% of the plastic in the Great Pacific Garbage Patch.

⚠ Our oceans are one of Earth's biggest carbon sinks, but bottom-trawling fishing boats disturb this important environment and release as much CO_2 as the entire aviation industry.

⚠ Just 56% of the vegetables and 16% of the fruit consumed in the UK is grown there.

⚠ Producing 1kg (2lb) of wheat requires 750 litres (165 gallons) of water, whereas 1kg of beef requires up to 100,000 litres (22,000 gallons).

⚠ The average cow expels around 200g (0.5lb) of methane each day, a gas even more potent than CO_2.

✅ Organic potatoes have significantly higher levels of vitamin C, magnesium, iron and phosphorous than non-organic equivalents.

✅ British organic farms contain 85% more plant species, 33% more bats, 17% more spiders and 5% more birds than non-organic ones.

✅ Organic produce contains less water than conventional equivalents, so you're getting more food for your money than you may think.

⚠ Between 1990 and 2016, the area of UK agricultural land treated with pesticides rose by 63%. The land is treated twice as often during the growing season – showing something needs to change.

...ghest ...growth in ...the organic ...12.6%, the ...try alone is ...2.79 billion.

...% of people think ...at governments and ...administration should provide more support to farmers using minimal or no pesticides.

FOOD CHAIN

The carbon footprint of food is affected not only by the distance it has travelled but also by the amount of energy required to produce it. Animal products, such as meat and dairy, are among the most resource-hungry items on the menu.

👍 **GO VEGAN** By trying a vegan, vegetarian or flexitarian diet, you can cut the CO_2 associated with your diet by up to half. You'll also be cutting down the water and land needed to produce your food – an ethical win-win! For every 500g (1lb) of beef you avoid you'll trim your carbon footprint by up to 6kg (12lb) of CO_2.

💲 **CUT DOWN ON FISH** As well as depleting fish stocks by overfishing, the fishing industry uses huge amounts of fuel for its trawlers, and dumped plastic fishing gear is one of the biggest ocean polluters. Help to reduce demand by reducing your consumption.

👍 **CHOOSE WELL** Everything we eat has an impact and even a vegan diet isn't perfect. When reducing your meat and dairy, try to avoid too many processed products or those which contain palm oil (it contributes to deforestation and has horrendous impacts on wildlife and communities). When it comes to milk, choose oat milk, one of the most sustainable dairy alternatives.

WHAT'S THE BEEF?
In the last 50 years, global meat production has increased five-fold and the amount of meat eaten per person has doubled. This has put a heavy burden on the environment, as it requires much more land and water, as well as about ten times more energy, to produce animal than vegetable protein. One of the biggest impacts of meat production is the large amount of methane expelled by livestock. Methane is around 21 times more potent as a greenhouse gas than CO_2, and 37% of human-created methane emissions come from the livestock sector. Add to this the collateral damage associated with deforestation for pasture, production of fertilizers for feed crops, and energy to run meatpacking plants, and the huge environmental and ethical impact of meat is undeniable.

Supermarket shopping can come at a high price to the environment:

- in order to provide large volumes of standard products, supermarkets tend to buy produce at rock-bottom prices, often from overseas suppliers
- even a product grown relatively locally may have travelled hundreds – or even thousands – of miles from farm to retail outlet via a number of different locations for processing, packaging, storage and distribution
- strict requirements for uniform appearance mean that large proportions of each crop are often rejected.

You can avoid the excessive costs (to both you and the environment) of buying from supermarkets and their middlemen by buying food directly from growers.

DIRECT BUYING

Popping to the supermarket is a convenient way to stock your cupboards, but the carbon impacts are high. Buying direct from producers can trim your groceries' carbon footprint and also save you money.

($) **SHOP AT A LOCAL FARMERS' MARKET** that restricts the provenance of produce on sale to a radius of 160 or even 80km (100 or 50 miles) – in contrast to the 1,600-km (1,000-mile) journey of the average supermarket item. Or seek out local farm shops to buy direct from the producer in situ.

($) **SIGN UP TO A BOX SCHEME** that sources and delivers organic, seasonal food within a limited radius. Look for a Community Supported Agriculture (CSA) farm in your area (see p.68).

($) **BEAUTY IS IN THE EYE OF THE STALLHOLDER** By insisting on "perfect" produce, supermarkets force farmers to waste huge amounts of delicious food – and the energy required to grow it. Let local traders know you're happy to buy "strange-looking" fruit and vegetables. You could also try a "wonky" veg or bread box scheme.

UK supermarkets produce about 5 million tonnes (5.5 million US tons) of greenhouse gases per year – almost 1% of total UK emissions.

It's estimated that for every tonne (2,200lb) of bananas shipped, 2 tonnes (4,400lb) of fruit are left behind on the plantations.

Increasing vegetable intake so that everybody in the UK eats their five-a-day could contribute eight extra months to the average life expectancy and decrease greenhouse gas emissions by over 8%.

Local veg box delivery schemes saw an increase in sales of 111% in spring 2020, during the COVID-19 lockdown.

2021 saw the h[...] year-on-year [...] 15 years for [...] market. U[...] UK indus[...] worth [...]

78[...]

ORGANIC PRODUCTS

Organic farming is experiencing a surge in popularity as consumers recognize the benefits of food produced without energy-intensive and biodiversity-destroying synthetic fertilizers and pesticides, plant-growth regulators and livestock-feed additives.

($) **DRINK ORGANIC MILK** If you can't switch all your food to organic, milk (ideally plant milk) is a good place to start. Organic milk uses only a third of the energy needed to produce the non-organic version and contains higher levels of nutrients.

($) **GET THE BALANCE RIGHT** Organic isn't always the best choice: highly packaged, air-freighted organic produce will ratchet up a hefty carbon footprint en route. Try to find food that's seasonal, local, unpackaged and unprocessed. And if it's also organic, that's even better! Also look for non-food organic products, including textiles (see p.82) and toiletries.

($) **NATURAL CHOICE** 75% of our food crops depend on pollinators like bees, and our soils are home to 25% of the earth's species. Choosing organic produce or growing your own organically helps to protect this vital biodiversity.

GREAT TASTE, LOW CO_2
Conventional farming uses huge amounts of fossil-fuel based fertilizer, which leads to the emission of significant levels of greenhouse gases in both its manufacture and application. In contrast, organic soils capture and store up to 30% more CO_2 than soils from conventional farms. If all the corn and soybeans grown in the US were farmed organically, 250 billion kg (550 billion lb) of CO_2 would be removed from the atmosphere each year.

One average-sized organic farm can absorb 120 cars' worth of CO_2.

If you're lucky enough to have a local veganic (vegan organic) farm, try to source its produce. Find out more via the Vegan Organic Network.

LOW-CO_2 TEXTILES
Look for items made from the following types of eco-friendly fibre:

- recycled materials – fleece jackets can be made from plastic, trainers from denim and car tyres, and handbags from otherwise wasted orange peels and pineapple leaves.
- organic cotton, jute, cork and linen
- bamboo or hemp fibre – these are both naturally fast-growing plants that absorb above-average levels of CO_2 and require minimal application of fertilizer and pesticides.

In contrast, avoid synthetic fabrics such as nylon and polyester, which are made from petrochemicals in very energy-intensive processes. Nylon manufacture produces nitrous oxide, a greenhouse gas 310 times more potent than CO_2.

CLOTHING

Sales may be tempting, especially with many chains claiming to have "green" clothing ranges. Choose carefully and look after your clothes to minimize the carbon emissions of looking good.

($) **BUY TO LAST** Choose well-made garments you really like and will wear for years – avoid fast fashion. Opt for vintage clothing – it's cheaper and often better made.

👍 **SWAP** Instead of splurging on new outfits, host a clothes-swapping party with your friends.

👍 **LOOK AFTER YOUR WARDROBE** Have clothes repaired or even restyled into new garments. Cut costs by finding out if you have a local repair café or community restart project.

👜
👍 **RECYCLE CLOTHES** that are beyond restyling or repair. They can be shredded and rewoven into new items through a textile-recycling scheme.

👍
($) **PROTECT WATERWAYS** While clothing made from recycled plastic bottles or marine waste is a brilliant example of recycling, remember that any plastic fibres shed harmful microplastics. Protect waterways by using a Guppyfriend bag, which traps microfibres when they leave your clothes in the washing machine.

A hectare (2.5 acres) of bamboo absorbs up to 2 tonnes (4,400lb) of CO_2 each year.

Wearing clothes for an extra 9 months reduces a garment's carbon, water and waste footprint by up to 30%.

It takes 10 times more energy to make a tonne (2,200lb) of textiles than the same amount of glass.

Wash clothes at a low temperature and avoid tumble drying (see p.60). This will help your clothes to last longer (and save electricity, of course).

If every Briton bought one recycled wool item a year instead of a new one, the energy saving would be equivalent to 4.5 billion days of an average family's electricity needs.

Non-organic cotton is the world's most polluting crop, accounting for up to a quarter of all agrichemical use, including 50,000 tonnes (55,000 US tons) of pesticides each year.

The average Western shopaholic adds more than 3 tonnes (6,600lb) of CO_2 to their carbon footprint each year simply by buying stuff. Without full "life cycle assessment", which looks at the impacts of every stage of a product's life, it can be very difficult to work out the relative carbon footprints of different items. But generally, when it comes to reducing the consumption component of your carbon footprint, less is definitely more. As well as avoiding over-packaged items and buying locally produced (ideally organic) produce, buying fewer, more durable things, reusing and repairing them and choosing second-hand where possible can cut the impacts of your buying habits dramatically.

In nature there's no such thing as waste – every natural material, once it's fulfilled one function, is useful in another way. With

BUYING LESS

Everything you buy in the shops, from radishes to hairclips, has taken energy to grow or extract, manufacture, package, transport and sell. So, by finding ways to curb your consumption, you can cut your carbon footprint.

 EAT BEFORE YOU SHOP FOR FOOD Studies show that this helps trim the amount you buy.

 THINK LONG-TERM Investing in high-quality durable goods is cheaper in the long run, and less wasteful than buying cheap, throw-away versions.

 BUY SERVICES RATHER THAN PRODUCTS – such as leasing services for office equipment so manufacturers produce durable, updatable products rather than ones that are obsolete in a few years.

 MAKE SURE NEW THINGS WILL LAST Check that items of hardware can be easily repaired and that the manufacturer will supply spare parts. It may be worth investing a little more in products with long guarantees.

AVOID DISPOSABLES, which invariably have a high carbon impact. For example: cover food with a plate, lid or reusable food wrap instead of foil or cling film; use handtowels and tea towels instead of kitchen paper; buy sturdy, reusable cutlery, crockery and drinking straws for barbecues and picnics; take reusable bags and produce bags to the shops; in the bathroom try reusables such as a safety razor, washable facial rounds or cloths, and a menstrual cup or pants; and when out and about, always carry a reusable water bottle and coffee cup.

DO SOME REAL FEEL-GOOD SHOPPING Massages, beauty treatments and concert tickets are great junk-free treats.

FIX THINGS rather than throwing them away at the first sign of wear or malfunction. Look for specialist menders in your area, or learn a new skill yourself, such as furniture upholstery or renovation. You may even have a local repair café or community restart project.

FIND A NEW LEASE OF LIFE Try selling unwanted items online (for example, on eBay), donating them to a new home (try Freecycle, OLIO or Craigslist) or swapping them with neighbours via a community swap shop. These forums could also help you find things you need.

easy access to plentiful goods, we tend to forget this basic principle, and we throw away 80% of all manufactured products we buy within six months of purchase. As well as reducing the amount you buy, think laterally and try to find as many uses as possible for everything you've bought before you throw it away.

THE 5 RS
When considering a purchase, keep the "5 Rs" in mind – refuse (say no to new), reuse (avoid disposables), repurpose (new ways to use what you already have), recycle (do this if the other "Rs" aren't feasible), and rot (composting natural matter).

Of household objects thrown away, an average of **40%** are beyond repair, **20%** need fixing and **40%** are still perfectly usable.

GREENER ONLINE SHOPPING

If you can't get the products you need locally, buying goods online can be an environmentally friendly and time-saving way to shop. When buying from the cyber aisles, minimize your environmental impact in the following ways:

- avoid requesting next-day delivery, as this requires energy-guzzling bespoke delivery trips
- combine orders with friends, relatives and colleagues to save on postage and unnecessary journeys
- have orders delivered to your workplace, where they can always be accepted – this avoids items having to be re-sent if you're not at home when they arrive
- work out sizes or specifications before ordering to avoid emissions from returns
- choose independent companies who use environmentally minded packaging and delivery.

INTERNET SHOPPING AND SERVICES

Take advantage of the huge range of services available online to cut emissions from trips to the shops and powering retail outlets, and save yourself time and money. Just remember to turn the device off when you've finished!

MANAGE YOUR FINANCES ONLINE Online bill-paying and banking help avoid unnecessary energy use from paper production, printing, postage and waste disposal. They also generate a lot less paperwork to clutter up your home.

INVEST IN INDEPENDENT Spend your money wisely by choosing independent, local and ethical retailers. For example, Bookshop.org allows you to support local bookshops while shopping online; and websites such as Etsy and Not On The Highstreet help you to support independent makers.

CHOOSE DOWNLOADS Stream or download music, television and films rather than buying plastic CDs and DVDs, or seek out second-hand discs.

Just 6–8% of clothing items purchased from a physical store are returned, compared to 30% of online orders.

 Is buying groceries online greener? It depends! Weigh up your delivery company's refrigeration method, packaging and transport type, and compare this with your local farm shop, supermarket or store of choice.

One delivery round by a supermarket delivery van can remove the need for 20 separate car journeys to the supermarket.

 20% of online shopping returns end up in landfill because they are unable to be resold by the retailer.

Change your online passwords regularly and trash unsolicited e-mails purporting to be from your bank that ask you to divulge sensitive information.

 If all Americans received and paid their bills online, they'd save 18.5 million trees' worth of paper each year.

On average, online shopping has a lower carbon footprint – but that doesn't take into account the impact of returns.

Packaging adds around 7% to the prices of supermarket items.

 Cans made from recycled, rather than new, aluminium use 95% less energy during production.

 2.5 billion disposable coffee cups are thrown away every year in the UK.

 The average person could cut their carbon emissions by 540kg (1,190lb) a year by reducing their packaging waste by 10%.

 Only 14% of plastic ever produced has been collected for recycling and just 5% has been successfully recycled.

 A robust, reusable bag needs to be used only 11 times to have a lower environmental impact than using 11 disposable plastic bags.

CUTTING THE WRAP

It's likely that a significant proportion of your household waste contents consists of food packaging. Before you even think about recycling (see pp.91–3), make sure you're avoiding as much waste as possible every time you shop.

($) **BUY NON-PERISHABLE ITEMS AND DRIED GOODS**, such as rice, lentils and pasta, in bulk. One large package requires less energy to make than a lot of small ones. Even better, buy them loose or from a zero-waste refill shop and put them in your own reusable containers.

($) **CHOOSE PRODUCTS SOLD IN REFILLABLE CONTAINERS**, and make the effort to reuse them. Ask your favourite brands and shops to stock this kind of packaging if they don't already.

👍 **GIVE IT BACK** Make your feelings known by unwrapping excessively packaged purchases and posting the packaging back to the manufacturers with a letter.

👍 **GO EASY ON THE FOIL** Aluminium production is resource- and energy-intensive. So use foil sparingly, reusing it where possible, and choose recycled foil. Then recycle it to recoup the valuable resources it contains.

MAKE DISPOSABLE BAGS HISTORY

Across the UK, the use of plastic shopping bags has dropped by 95% since a charge was introduced. The benefits are already seen and scientists found 30% fewer plastic bags on the seabed. Before the charge, the average person used 140 plastic bags per year. Despite research showing that the average household already had 40 plastic bags, their usage had continued to rise.

It takes 11 barrels of crude oil to produce a tonne (2,200lb) of plastic bags, but paper bags aren't much better – it takes 17 trees to produce a tonne (2,200lb) of them.

Bring your own canvas bags with you every time you shop. Using your own bag instead of just a modest four disposable plastic bags per week will cut your annual carbon footprint by about 8kg (18lb).

Certified compostable carrier bags made from

maize or potato starch are a better option than normal plastic bags. In the right conditions, they break down into harmless elements rather than lingering for hundreds of years like their petrochemical counterparts. However, their manufacture still uses large amounts of energy and other resources, so you're really much better off with a reusable bag whenever possible.

 AVOID PACKAGING MADE FROM MIXED MATERIALS, such as plastic and foil or Tetra Paks – these are harder to recycle.

 REUSE PLASTIC CONTAINERS from take-away meals or from store-bought foods.

 AVOID SINGLE SACHETS The packaging and processing that goes into them gives them a huge environmental footprint – an individual serving of coffee has ten times as much packaging as the equivalent coffee sold in bulk.

 PACK YOUR OWN LUNCH in reusable containers. You'll save money and avoid generating 200g (½lb) or more of empty single-serve yoghurt pots, juice cartons and sandwich bags each day.

 AVOID POLYSTYRENE – it's made from petrochemicals and doesn't biodegrade; and because it's so bulky, transportation and processing are expensive, so widespread recycling is unlikely to be feasible.

THANK COMPANIES that have switched to more compact, biodegradable or recycled packaging.

RECYCLING

Everything you throw away has a carbon footprint – created through its production and ultimately its disposal. So try to reduce the amount you throw away – by buying less and reusing things, and following the 5 Rs (p.85) as much as possible.

👍 **KEEP A LOW PROFILE** The average adult receives 19kg (42lb) of unsolicited mail a year. Register with a mail preference service, telling them you wish to opt out of "door to door" leaflets, and always tick the "don't pass on my address" box when filling out forms.

👍 **SHARE NEWSPAPERS AND MAGAZINES** with colleagues or neighbours rather than always buying your own, and try to find a second use for them – for example, as wrapping paper – before you recycle them.

👍 **TURN OVER AN OLD LEAF** Every tonne (2,200lb) of paper reused or recycled avoids the emission of over a tonne (2,200lb) of CO_2, keeps 3 cubic metres (105 cubic feet) of waste out of landfill, saves enough energy to light the average home for six months and leaves 17 trees standing, busy absorbing CO_2.

👍 **BE VIRTUOUS WITH YOUR VITREOUS** Recycling just one glass bottle saves enough energy to power a television for 90 minutes.

THE BENEFITS OF RECYCLING
Recycling helps reduce greenhouse gas emissions in a whole host of ways – some less obvious than others:

- It diverts organic waste from landfills, avoiding the production of methane (a greenhouse gas 21 times more potent than CO_2), which is released when organic matter decomposes anaerobically (without oxygen).

- It cuts down on incineration, reducing greenhouse gas emissions from the combustion of waste.

- It saves energy – reusing products or making them with recycled rather than virgin materials requires less energy for extraction, transportation, processing and manufacturing, so less CO_2 is emitted. For example, recycled glass uses up to 50% less energy, recycled paper products around 60–70% less energy, and recycled aluminium a whopping 95% less energy than their equivalents made from virgin materials.

- It increases storage of carbon in trees – plants absorb CO_2 from the atmosphere and store it, a process called carbon sequestration. Waste prevention and recycling of paper products allow more trees to remain standing in the forest, where they can continue removing CO_2 from the atmosphere.

Up to 80% of the average amount of household waste can be recycled. For every kilo (2lb) of waste you recycle, you can reduce CO_2 emissions by at least the same amount. If you're currently pretty wasteful, cutting back and recycling could cut your annual carbon footprint by up to a tonne (2,200lb).

👍 **RECYCLE PLASTIC BOTTLES** Plastic is difficult to recycle, since it comes in so many different forms, or polymers. But with a third of world oil production expected to be linked to plastics by 2030, we need to recoup what we can. Avoid single use plastic wherever possible and recycle, reuse and repurpose your plastics. PET plastic bottles (identified by a number 1 inside a triangle) are a good place to start – recycling just one saves enough energy to power a 14W compact fluorescent lightbulb for over 25 hours.

👍 **YES CAN DO** Producing an aluminium can from recycled material takes only 5% of the energy needed to make it from virgin raw materials – recycling just one can saves enough energy to run a computer for three hours.

👍 **RECYCLE THE "UNRECYCLABLE"** See what TerraCycle schemes are available in your area – a way of recycling items such as plastic tablet packaging, contact lenses, crisp packets and electric toothbrush heads.

💲 **BUY RECYCLED PRODUCTS** such as recycled paper or toilet paper, recycled aluminium foil and clothing made from recycled fibres.

👍 **SPEAK OUT** Ask suppliers to design packaging that is minimal and can be reused and/or recycled.

In the US, the amount of aluminium thrown away could rebuild the country's entire commercial air fleet every three months.

It takes 70% less energy to recycle paper than it does to make it new from raw materials.

Every year the UK needs a forest the size of Wales to provide all its paper.

Remember to keep the "5 Rs" in mind – refuse, reuse, repurpose, recycle and rot (see p. 85).

The average dustbin (trash can) contains enough unrealized energy for 500 baths each year.

The global aluminium industry uses as much electric power as the continent of Africa.

8 million tonnes (9 million US tons) of the world's plastics end up in our oceans each year, creating a garbage patch three times the size of France.

Recycling just two glass bottles saves enough energy to boil water to make five cups of tea.

THE BIG NAPPY DEBATE

Opinions vary about the environmental impacts of disposable versus reusable nappies (diapers). The devil's in the detail, so whichever you choose, make sure you're minimizing their impact:

- Reusable nappies score well on waste, but require a lot of energy for washing, so choose the lowest temperature possible, and avoid using the tumble dryer. Even better, use a nappy-laundering service, which is more efficient than home washing. Try before you buy by contacting a cloth nappy library.

- Disposable nappies require huge amounts of oil, paper and plastic. If you use disposables, choose a brand that uses materials from sustainable forests or, even better, a biodegradable nappy – but make sure you compost them appropriately, as they won't break down in landfill.

BABYCARE

It's a touchy subject, but having children adds enormously to our impact on the planet – particularly in the West, where our carbon footprints are already huge. If you do have children, bring them up to tread lightly on the Earth.

👍 **PACKAGING-FREE MILK!** If it's an option, breast milk is healthier not only for your baby but also for the environment. It comes without any packaging, and doesn't require fossil-fuel energy to make!

👍 **MAKE YOUR OWN ORGANIC BABYFOOD** using locally (or home-) grown fruit and vegetables. A batch of pureed fruit and veg frozen in small containers will last for ages. It will be fresher, cheaper and tastier than shop-bought versions, and is quick and easy to make.

💲 **LEND, BORROW AND SWAP BABY EQUIPMENT** Babies grow out of clothes and other equipment at an alarming rate – usually well before they're worn out. Bargains are often available in charity shops (thrift stores) and nearly new sales and on websites such as Freecycle and eBay.

Studies suggest that about 70% of parents become more interested in environmental issues following the birth of their baby.

In the Netherlands disposable nappies are composted in industrial systems and the resulting methane is collected for use as fuel.

Use washable baby wipes – either bought or home-made from old fabric – rather than disposables.

If every child in America were bottle-fed, almost 86,000 tonnes (95,000 US tons) of tin plate would be needed to produce 550 million cans of formula powder each year.

Using reusable nappies during the first 2½ years of your baby's life generates around 570kg (1,260lb) of greenhouse gases; using disposables generates about 650kg (1,400lb).

Babies typically get through more than 5,000 nappies before they're toilet trained.

Disposable nappies take up to 500 years to decompose, and it takes a cup of crude oil to produce the plastic for just one nappy – around 8 barrels of oil per child.

 Nappy-laundering services use around 30% less energy and 40% less water than home washing.

The UK's toy industry is worth £2.1 billion a year.

 The average American child receives 69 new toys each year.

 Americans purchase around 5 billion batteries each year and produce around 150,000 tonnes (165,000 US tons)of battery waste annually.

 Look for toys, such as DIY solar-power kits and hydrogen model cars, designed to educate and inspire children about low-carbon technologies.

TOYS

Think hard before you buy the latest in-vogue, short-lived plaything for your children – perhaps there's something much simpler that would be more fun for them and less harmful to the planet.

($) **BUY SECOND-HAND TOYS** Check out eBay, Craigslist, Freecycle, Facebook, yard sales, or your local classifieds for nearly new bargains.

($) **WOOD'S GOOD** Buy FSC (Forest Stewardship Council)-accredited wooden toys. They'll last generations longer than the cheap plastic stuff.

👍 **JOIN A TOY LIBRARY** to give your children more toys than they could possibly get bored with. Alternatively, start your own toy-sharing circle with friends who have children.

👍 **SPARK YOUR CHILD'S IMAGINATION** by giving them everyday items like cardboard boxes, fabric offcuts, shells or pieces of wood to adapt into their own toys or craft projects, providing hours more fun than manufactured toys.

POWER DOWN
A seemingly unavoidable feature of modern childhood, electronic toys are usually made from petrochemical-based plastics. They create significant carbon emissions in their manufacture and produce yet more in their use and disposal. If your child is truly desperate for an electronic toy:

- try to choose one that's well made and won't break within weeks
- ideally, find a toy or game that can be varied or upgraded (for example, a console that plays a number of different games which can be swapped with friends)
- invest in a set of rechargeable batteries and a charger – ideally a solar-powered one
- teach your child(ren) to switch off the toy whenever they're not using it.

JOIN THE CHAIN GANG

Walking and cycling are both great for avoiding unnecessary carbon emissions, getting your kids fit and healthy, and having fun!

- Teach a child to ride a bike. Every 6-km (4-mile) trip by bike rather than car avoids about 1kg (2lb) of CO_2 emissions and builds a strong heart – research shows that regular cyclists tend to be as fit as people 10 years younger who don't do regular exercise.
- If you don't feel confident about you or your children cycling on roads, enrol in a family cycling proficiency class to build up your skills and road awareness.
- Organize family bike rides or walks during your free time and explore parts of your neighbourhood, and pockets of flora and fauna, you'd never know existed if you were sitting in a car.

GOOD HABITS

Avoid scaring your children with apocalyptic horror stories about the daunting challenges facing the planet; instead, help them to understand how to reduce their carbon footprint by teaching them some good habits.

TEAM EFFORT Put your children in charge of some carbon-cutting tasks around the home – for example, checking that lights and appliances are switched off, looking after the composting or sorting waste for recycling – and reward them for doing well. If you make these chores into enjoyable activities, the habits are likely to last a lifetime.

GET YOUR KIDS GARDENING Encourage them to cultivate some of their favourite fruit and vegetables from scratch – and super-locally. Grow strawberries in pots, plant tomatoes in grow-bags or sow a patch of salad seeds.

COOKERY MASTER-CLASS Show your children what to do with their harvest by asking them to help you prepare nutritious meals made from fresh ingredients using energy-efficient techniques (see pp.43–4). Instilling in your children the ability to cook will make them less likely to resort to over-processed, over-packaged ready meals when they've flown the nest.

ASK YOUR CHILD'S SCHOOL FOR BIKE SHELTERS In Denmark 60% of children cycle to school. Encourage your local school to move toward this target by providing secure, covered shelters for pupils and staff.

WALK THE BUS TO SCHOOL Try organizing a "walking bus" for your children and their friends rather than driving them. It's more sociable, keeps your children healthy and reduces the number of cars on the road, making life safer for everyone.

TOYLESS BUT NOT JOYLESS Encourage your children to have fun without play equipment – plant trees with them, or teach them simple games like hopscotch or hide and seek. Studies show that children who regularly play in natural environments are healthier, more agile and better coordinated than their indoor counterparts.

• Cycle or walk your kids to school. With a pepped-up metabolism and fresh air in their lungs, they'll be fitter and more alert than their car-borne peers. And by staying out of your car, you'll avoid adding to CO_2 emissions and congestion. By switching from the car to a carbon-free school run, you'd avoid around 30–40kg (65–90lb) of emissions a month for a 5-km (3-mile) round trip twice a day.

At 8.50am, one in five cars on the road in UK towns and cities are taking children to school.

POWER SAVE

Only about 15% of the $250 billion-worth of power used by computers worldwide each year is spent actually computing – the rest is wasted idling. Use your computer smartly to minimize its electricity consumption:

- set your device to enter power-saving mode after 10 minutes of inactivity – this could cut its energy use by 60–70%
- shut your device down if you're not going to be using it for more than an hour or two – it's a myth that computers use a lot of power to start up
- don't leave it on overnight, or you'll waste enough energy to laser print around 800 A4 pages
- unplug your computer at the end of the day – it uses a small amount of electricity (about 8W) even when fully shut down.

TECHNOLOGY

Computers may be great inventions, but the modern-day dependence on them is fast becoming an environmental scourge: globally the IT industry accounts for around 3.7% of CO_2 emissions – about the same as aviation.

($) **CHOOSE A MODEL** that can be easily upgraded or repaired and so is less likely to become obsolete in the blink of an eye.

($) **MAKE YOUR NEXT COMPUTER A LAPTOP** – it will consume up to 90% less energy than a desktop computer.

($) **THE CLICK OF A BUTTON** Every act we perform online has an impact. The energy needed to run your device, and to power networks, data centres and vast servers all add up. Try to tread lightly online by only streaming videos when you're connected to Wi-Fi, unsubscribing from unwanted emails, cutting down emails with large attachments and using an ethical search engine such as Ecosia.

(👍) **SECOND LIFE** When they're really no longer useful, give your computer, tablet or phone to one of the many organizations that now recondition IT equipment for reuse by non-profit bodies such as schools or charities.

A spam email creates 0.3g (¹⁄₁₀₀ oz) CO_2e, while the average email or WhatsApp message creates 4g (¹⁄₁₀ oz) CO_2e and those with large attachments or photos create 50g (2lb) CO_2e. Time to get unsubscribing!

If every adult in the UK sent one less "thank you" email, it could save 16,433 tonnes (18,000 US tons) of carbon a year – the equivalent of taking over 3,000 diesel cars off the road.

The average PC takes around 1.8 tonnes (4,000lb) of chemicals, fossil fuels and water to produce, generates around 100kg (220lb) of CO_2 per year and is junked after 3 years.

Video conferencing, such as Zoom, produces just 7% of the emissions of meeting in person.

If you upgrade your existing computer rather than buying a new one, you could save around 250kg (550lb) of fossil fuel.

60% of the world's Internet traffic and roughly 1% of global emissions come from watching videos online.

Browsing the Internet on a phone over a mobile network is at least twice as energy intensive as using it over Wi-Fi.

The plastic alone in each PC system requires about 7 litres (1½ gallons) of crude oil to make.

The paper industry is the greatest industrial consumer of water. It takes 300 litres (66 gallons) of water to make 1kg (2lb) of paper.

Inkjet printers use 10–15W, but laser printers use 60–100W. Even when on standby, laser printers can consume 30–35% of their peak power requirements.

The average Briton uses around 200kg (440lb) of paper each year and only 40% of this is recycled.

Printer toner cartridges can be reused up to seven times.

Look for photocopiers with an "auto off" feature. This could reduce the copier's energy consumption by up to 60%.

If everyone worked from home for one day a week, it would save 1% of global oil use for road transport each year. Although this increases our energy use at home, it would still save the equivalent of Greater London's annual CO_2 emissions.

OFFICE EQUIPMENT AND SUPPLIES

Think carefully about how you use the clever kit filling your office to ensure that your nine-to-five is as efficient and climate-friendly as possible.

👍 **SHARE-WARE** If your organization shares office space with others, club together to share larger pieces of equipment, such as photocopiers.

💲 **IF YOU NEED A NEW PRINTER, BUY A DUPLEX MODEL**, which prints on both sides, halving paper use and reducing energy consumption by around 25%. Choose an inkjet printer, if possible, as they use much less energy than laser printers. If you need a laser printer, choose one with an energy-saving feature. This reduces energy use when idle by over 65%.

💲 **BUY RECYCLED PRINTER CARTRIDGES** This will save around a litre (⅕ gallon) of oil per cartridge.

💲 **DITCH SINGLE-USE** Around 70% of office waste is recyclable. Encourage your company to provide sufficient recycling facilities, such as separate bins for paper, plastic, food waste and aluminium. Could coffee grounds be composted, disposable cups ditched, and plastic milk containers replaced with glass bottles?

BE A PAPER MISER

Theoretically, many offices are now "paperless", encouraging people to communicate via computer rather than the printed word. But in reality, paper still represents more than 70% of office waste. So try to get the most out of every scrap:

- use both sides of the paper – you'll get through half the volume of wood and other resources used to make it, cutting CO_2 emissions by 2.5kg (5½lb) for every kilo of paper you save
- buy recycled printer paper and other stationery – you'll prevent more than 2kg (4½lb) of CO_2 emissions with every ream
- before sending a document to print, run spell check and verify print settings carefully to minimize wasted printouts
- read e-mails on screen – don't print them out unless really necessary, and then print only the section you need.

WHERE DO WE START?
If you're lucky enough to work for an organization with comprehensive environmental policies, make sure you know what they are and contribute to making them work – otherwise they're just another piece of (wasted) paper.

If your company is at a less advanced stage, the first thing it should do is carry out a carbon audit to quantify the nature and scale of its impacts. This should look at in-house energy use (by means of energy monitors on different types of equipment and analysis of energy bills) and other CO_2-generating activities such as travel, catering and ordering office supplies. Specialist footprinting organizations can help with all the carbon counting, and companies can join schemes such as WWF Green Office, 1% For The Planet and The Planet Mark.

CORPORATE ENERGY-SAVING

Don't save all the good work for home – your employer could save huge amounts of energy through company-wide carbon-cutting programmes, so do what you can to get the ball rolling.

SWITCH OFF LIGHTS AND EQUIPMENT WHEN NOT IN USE To cut out the human element, install automatic PC-shutdown software with power-saving mode and movement sensors to ensure lights are in operation only when needed. Close programmes when they're not in use, dim your screens and replace screensavers with standby mode – saving energy and money.

SMART HEATING AND COOLING Take a fresh look at the way your company heats and cools its premises and suggest ways to save energy and money. Don't heat or cool storerooms and corridors unnecessarily, keep doors closed and switch from rigidly seasonal heating to a "smart" scheme, which reflects the prevailing temperature and is turned down at weekends, at night and on holidays.

LOW-ENERGY COMMUTING Ask your employer to help workers use less energy for their commute by organizing lift-share schemes (see p.120), encouraging employees to work from home, providing showers and cycle storage, and gradually reducing parking spaces.

BEAM ME UP Next time you're faced with a long journey to a short meeting, think hard about whether you really need to be there in person. Video conferencing saves money and time, and avoids carbon-heavy travel.

SEND PARCELS BY BIKE Send deliveries around town quickly and cleanly using a cycle courier service. Completely carbon-neutral, bikes can nip between jammed traffic, making them the swiftest option for urban businesses, as well as helping to improve air quality.

BUY ENERGY-EFFICIENT EQUIPMENT AND APPLIANCES such as bulbs and computers (see pp.100–103), and make sure they're well maintained.

GIVE YOURSELF A BREAK Governments are increasingly using tax breaks to reward businesses that save energy and levies to penalize energy-wasters. Make sure that your organization is fully aware of how it can benefit.

Lighting an average-sized office overnight wastes enough energy to make 1,000 hot drinks.

Once your organization knows the nature of the challenge that it faces, it needs to agree a series of meaningful goals and put together short- and long-term action plans for achieving them. Successful corporate energy-saving programmes tend to do the following:

- clearly communicate the practical benefits of saving energy, using simple, memorable messages displayed consistently across a variety of media, including posters, company website and bulletin boards
- encourage suggestions from employees of all levels, so that the whole workforce has a strong sense of involvement
- recognize and reward employee participation
- provide regular updates on progress
- hold special events, such as open discussion forums, employee awareness days and inter-departmental energy-saving competitions.

JOIN A GREEN GYM

Rather than driving to an air-conditioned gym to work out on energy-hungry machines, why not get fit in nature? Get in touch with a local environmental group and volunteer for carbon-absorbing projects such as tree planting, hedge laying and developing school nature areas. In the UK you can join a Green Gym®, which builds in warm-ups before these productive outdoor workouts. GoodGym hosts groups of runners who combine exercise with giving back to the local community; and the Charity Miles app helps you raise money for charity every time you jog or hike.

GREAT OUTDOORS

Take your exercise into nature by using a free outdoors gym in parks and green spaces. Walking, cycling, wild swimming and stand-up paddleboarding can all be combined with a beach clean, river clean or litter pick to help give back.

SPORTS AND EXERCISE

A burgeoning fitness industry is encouraging us to improve the health of our bodies, but unfortunately much of what's on offer isn't so great for the health of the planet. Rethink your exercise routine to trim some carbon kilos.

 BUILD EXERCISE INTO YOUR DAILY ROUTINE
For example, take the stairs instead of the lift (elevator), carry your recycling to the local depot, and walk, run or cycle to work, to go shopping and to see friends.

RENT OR BORROW SPORTS EQUIPMENT, unless you use it regularly, to avoid wasting valuable resources on stuff that's only going to collect dust in a cupboard most of the time.

 RECYCLE YOUR TRAINERS when they're worn out. The rubber in their soles has a multitude of uses, including all-weather sports pitches.

 POOL CARE If you've got a swimming pool, fill it with filtered rainwater, heat it using solar-thermal panels, keep it covered to reduce heat loss, and check it regularly for leaks.

Cross-country skiing has a lower impact than downhill skiing because it doesn't require chairlifts (or the razing of a mountainside to make way for pistes).

The average golf course uses 100 times more water than a four-bedroomed home. Make sure your golf club irrigates sparingly and uses reclaimed water.

Ten gym treadmills use an average of 13,500kWh of electricity each month – enough to run your hair dryer non-stop for more than a year.

Covering a swimming pool with an insulating layer can reduce heat loss by as much as 30%.

Taking the train instead of a plane from London to Paris produces 90% less CO_2 emissions.

 Before you go away, remember to turn off your home heating (or air conditioning), or just leave it on a minimum freeze-guard setting.

 Once you've reached your destination, consider hiring bicycles instead of the usual rentacar.

A 100-room hotel could save more than 300,000 litres (66,000 gallons) of water a year through a linen and towel reuse programme.

The average hotel guest uses more than twice the amount of water they'd normally use at home.

HOTELS AND HOLIDAYS

Choose a staycation, slow travel or a destination close to home, using low-carbon transport and conserving energy once you're there. It's possible to spoil yourself without spoiling the planet.

👍 **STAY IN YOUR OWN CONTINENT**, and avoid long-haul flights, which can produce more CO_2 emissions per passenger than the average motorist does in a year. Choose direct flights – take-off consumes the most fuel. When possible, travel by rail, sea or road and embrace the journey as part of the adventure. Pack lightly and travel in economy class – less weight equals less fuel used!

💲 **SUPPORT LOW-CARBON RESORTS** Make a donation to the Travel Foundation (www. thetravelfoundation.org.uk), which funds carbon-reduction strategies such as energy-efficiency programmes for tourist accommodation in resorts worldwide.

👍 **THINK LOCALLY ON HOLIDAY** Choose local food specialities, which are fresher and tastier than anything imported. The poorest countries experience the worst effects of the climate crisis so consider volunteering while abroad. Avoid travel hotspots and visit developing countries for a significant time, supporting local communities whose livelihoods depend on tourists.

LOW-CARBON HOTELS
Make your next hotel stay as energy-efficient as possible:
- find a hotel with genuine green credentials – look for one belonging to the Green Tourism Business Scheme or the International Business Leaders Forum Tourism Partnership or one that's Energy Star-approved
- turn heating or air conditioning off, or at least down, unless it's really necessary and switch off lights and appliances when they're not needed
- take showers not baths
- ask to keep the same towels and sheets for several nights rather than having them changed daily
- talk to the manager about the hotel's environmental policies and suggest improvements – for example, installing energy-saving lightbulbs, using refillable toiletry containers, or using a renewable energy supply.

Make your special day really special by minimizing its environmental impact:

- source local products – particularly food, drink and flowers
- rent linens, furniture, glasses, and so on, rather than buying them
- look for organic, recycled or vintage outfits for a unique, low-impact look
- avoid supporting the energy-intensive mining of heavy metals by choosing antique rings
- select an easily accessible venue and encourage your guests to travel there by low-carbon forms of transport
- ask guests to take leftover flowers, food and drinks home at the end
- ask for gifts that will help support your low-carbon life together, such as bikes, fruit trees or public transport passes. Or set up an online donation registry to a charity running low-carbon projects.

CELEBRATIONS

Everyone loves a fantastic party. Next time you're organizing a celebration, make it one to remember by employing some low-carbon party-planning techniques.

CELEBRATE EARTH DAY every 22nd April.

MAKE LOW-IMPACT DECORATIONS, such as paper chains from magazines or Christmas tree decorations from a stiff dough of flour, water and a little salt, baked and decorated with colourful trimmings.

USE LED FAIRY LIGHTS, which consume up to 95% less energy than traditional bulbs.

GIVE LESS "STUFF" Instead of more potential landfill, give people experiences or services – tickets to an event, a meal out or a certificate for a massage. When you do give objects, wrap them in newspaper, fabric gift wrap or recycled wrapping paper tied with ribbons – so the paper can be used again.

AVOID SINGLE-USE plastic balloons, plates, cups and cutlery at parties. Instead, use crockery from home. If you really can't face the washing-up, choose compostable alternatives to plastic and ensure they are disposed of correctly.

⚠️ In the UK 2 million tonnes (over 2 million US tons) of CO_2 are emitted from transporting flowers just for Valentine's Day.

⚠️ The average UK wedding generates around 15 tonnes (33,000lb) of CO_2.

⚠️ The ingredients for a typical Christmas dinner travel up to 48,000km (30,000 miles).

 Over 30,000 balloons are found on US beaches every year. They can travel thousands of miles; and birds, turtles and other wildlife often mistake them for food, which can harm or even kill them.

⚠️ A typical string of Christmas tree lights left on for 10 hours a day over the Christmas period produces enough CO_2 to fill 50 party balloons.

The League of American Bicyclists awards Bicycle-Friendly Community status to US municipalities that actively support cycling, with 487 communities in 2021.

Replace an 8-km (5-mile) car trip with a bike ride once a week. This will prevent around 100kg (220lb) of CO_2 emissions a year – equivalent to watching TV solidly for 75 days.

It costs an average of £2,200 a year to run a car in the UK, taking into account factors such as fuel cost, insurance, servicing and road tax.

As of 2021, London's Santander Cycles have over 750 docking stations across the capital and 14,000 bikes to hire.

In Copenhagen, Denmark, ranked one of the happiest countries in the world, 62% of commuters travel by bicycle.

Cycling for half an hour a day can increase life expectancy by up to 4 years.

During the COVID-19 lockdown, more people embraced going off-road – 31% of Londoners chose walking over a different mode of transport; and 57% of people say they now go on more walks or walk for longer than they did before the pandemic.

USING YOUR LEGS

Over half the oil extracted worldwide is used for transport, a major cause of CO_2 emissions. To slow down the burn, use your legs to walk or cycle wherever and whenever you can. You'll benefit the health of both you and the planet.

USE A SMART WATCH, such as a Fitbit, or an app, such as Strava, to track your exercise. Research shows that the famous goal of 10,000 steps a day can provide great motivation, but the long-term health benefits of walking actually kick in at around 7,500 daily steps.

KIT YOUR BIKE OUT FOR CARGO Buy a basket for the front of your bicycle and some strong panniers for the back. If cycling is too much, try an e-bike rather than jumping in the car.

SHARE A BIKE Use city bike-hire schemes such as Vélib' in Paris, Call-a-Bike in Germany, Santander Cycles in London and OYBike throughout the UK. Ask your local authority for a similar scheme if there isn't one in your area.

FOLLOW THE TRAIL Ask your national cycling association for a map of local cycle routes.

GET A JOB CLOSE TO HOME, so you can walk or cycle to work for a carbon-free commute.

A DECONGESTANT THAT WORKS!

Congestion charging, a system involving charging drivers a fee to enter a designated zone during peak periods, has been a real success story in cities such as London, Singapore and Stockholm. In London, for example, the congestion charge has encouraged 500,000 motorists a day to leave their cars at home and travel into the city centre by foot, bicycle or public transport. Carbon emissions are down 16%, traffic delays have been cut by over 20%, and the local economy is thriving. Such strategies generate significant revenue to invest in public transport and walking and cycling schemes. Why not lobby your local authority to consider congestion charging for your home town?

The true fuel efficiency of a vehicle depends on the number of passengers it's carrying, a figure expressed in terms of "passenger km per litre"/"passenger miles per gallon" (pkpl/pmpg: vehicle efficiency multiplied by number of passengers). So, for example, the typical car averaging 13kpl (30mpg) and carrying two passengers is doing 26pkpl (60pmpg), whereas a bus that averages 2.5kpl (6mpg) while carrying 40 passengers is doing 100 pkpl (240pmpg) – four times as efficient as the car.

The French TGV high-speed train can travel at an average speed of more than 240kph (150mph).

PUBLIC TRANSPORT

If your trip's too long, you've got too much to carry, or the weather's too ghastly to walk or cycle, using public transport is a lower-carbon way of getting around than driving your car.

CELEBRATE WORLD CAR-FREE DAY, which is held each year on 22nd September, by leaving your car at home for 24 hours. If you normally commute by car, use this day to try out an alternative way to get to work. Taking the bus for a 24-km (15-mile) round trip to work each day could cut your carbon footprint by as much as 1.5 tonnes (3,300lb) of CO_2 per year.

ADJUST YOUR WORKING HOURS, if you can, so that you don't have to travel on public transport during peak times. That way the journey will be quicker and you'll be guaranteed a seat.

GET A MULTI-PURPOSE TRAVEL CARD, if they're available where you live, so you can take advantage of public transport as the mood strikes you and always get the best deal.

JUMP ON A BUS and you'll help to empty the roads. A bus can carry the occupants of 20 cars, producing far less pollution and taking up far less tarmac space.

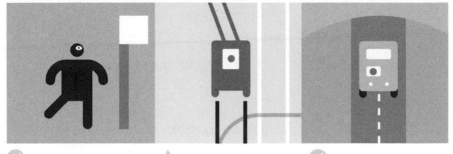

✓ The Bogotá rapid transit system in Colombia carries 1,600 passengers per bus per day and has achieved a 32% reduction in journey time and a 40% reduction in greenhouse-gas emissions.

✓ Public transport generates 95% less carbon monoxide and 50% less carbon dioxide and nitrogen oxide per passenger mile than private cars.

⚠ Carbon emissions per passenger per 1,600km (1,000 miles) vary greatly:
Coach – 122kg (270lb)
Intercity train – 204kg (450lb)
Small car – 268kg (590lb)
Aeroplane – 440kg (970lb)
4-wheel drive – 712kg (1,570lb).

✓ If all the UK's car drivers switched to public transport, CO_2 emissions from transport would be reduced by 90%.

✓ Ask your government to redress the balance in favour of public transport by increasing the cost of driving private cars and using the revenue to fund improved public transport.

⚠ Drivers in America's most congested cities spend more than 40 hours a year (an entire working week) sitting in stationary traffic.

BREAKING THE CHAIN

The shape of the developed world has been heavily influenced by the car. Out-of-town shopping centres and supermarkets are supplanting the town-centre shopping districts, meaning that it's hard not to drive on a regular basis. The average shopping trip in Britain is 7km (4.3 miles) – too far for most people to walk when carrying heavy bags.

It'll be a hard trend to reverse, but designing communities with shops within walking or cycling distance and well served by public transport is key to making low-carbon living a reality. Cities worldwide are taking up the challenge. Bogotá in Colombia and Curitiba in Brazil have bus rapid transit systems with exclusive routes for buses (the inspiration for the Los Angeles Orange Line), and many cities, including London and Stockholm, use congestion charging (see p.113).

TAKE THE TRAIN – a great way to travel long distances with minimal environmental impact. Unlike flying, you don't have to waste time checking in hours before departure, and, unlike driving, you can get stuff done en route – even if only catching up on some sleep!

SAVE A COACHLOAD OF CARBON Travelling long distance by coach is an even lower carbon option than train travel – switching from car to coach can cut the CO_2 produced by your journey by up to 90%.

CYCLE TO THE STATION OR BUS STOP to speed up your journey door to door. Encourage your public-transport service to provide bike racks if they don't already (ask them to look at bicycle-friendly cities like Copenhagen for inspiration), or buy a folding bicycle which you can take onboard and then unfold for a quick getaway at the other end.

Better air quality, safer roads, healthier communities, quieter neighbourhoods and less congestion are just a few of the benefits to having fewer cars on the roads.

ECO DRIVING

Transport is now the UK's largest source of greenhouse gases, with 56% of emissions coming from cars. The way in which we maintain and drive our cars has a huge impact on fuel efficiency.

👍 **SLOW DOWN!** Faster driving uses more fuel, so try to exert gentle pressure on the accelerator and keep speeds down to maximize your kpl/mpg.

👍 **AVOID EXCESS WEIGHT OR DRAG**, as it costs you fuel. Leave the roof rack behind and take heavy items (golf clubs etc.) out of the boot if you're not using them. Carrying an extra 50kg (110lb) can reduce fuel efficiency by up to 2%.

👍 **GET YOUR CAR SERVICED REGULARLY** This should pay for itself in saved fuel. An inefficient, poorly maintained engine can reduce your car's fuel efficiency by 10% or more.

👍 **USE THE RIGHT GEAR** Move up to top gear as soon as possible without accelerating harder than necessary. However, avoid allowing the engine to labour in a high gear when you're going uphill, as this will use more fuel and put stress on the engine. If you're driving an automatic, ease back slightly on the accelerator as the car gathers momentum so that the transmission can shift up quickly and smoothly.

THINK BEFORE YOU DRIVE

Journeys of less than 3km (2 miles) cause the most pollution per km/mile: a straining, cold engine produces 60% more emissions than a warm one. So, before you jump in the car, ask yourself whether you really need to drive. If you can, time your car journeys to avoid rush hour – sitting in traffic, your fuel efficiency goes down to zero kpl/mpg. Combine various errands into a single trip and you'll save time, effort and money.

As well as sticking to a regular professional car servicing and tuning schedule, there are a number of key maintenance tasks you can undertake to improve your car's fuel performance:

- Maintain the correct tyre pressures – ideally, check your tyres every week or two. Driving with under-inflated tyres increases resistance against the road, which makes the engine work harder and use more fuel. It will also increase the rate of tyre wear and affect the car's handling.
- Check your oil level, and use the recommended grade of oil. A well-lubricated engine uses less fuel.
- Look out for oil leaks, and get them fixed immediately.
- Replace clogged air filters, which reduce engine efficiency. In polluted regions, filters become blocked more quickly.

SMOOTHLY DOES IT Studies have shown that an aggressive driving style characterized by sharp acceleration, high speeds and hard braking reduces travel time by only 4% on average, while increasing fuel consumption by up to 40%. Avoid unnecessarily marked changes of speed by keeping your distance from the vehicle in front, slowing down gradually when approaching junctions and red lights, and keeping overtaking to a minimum. Nearly 50% of cars on UK motorways are exceeding the 70 mph limit, but if we all stuck to the speed limit this would cut 1% of annual road transport emissions.

LAY OFF THE AIR CON, because using it can increase fuel consumption by more than 20% in city driving. Unless it's stiflingly hot, wind down the windows instead. If you're travelling faster than 72kph (45mph), it's more efficient to use your car's flow-through ventilation than to wind down the windows, because at higher speeds open windows increase the drag on the car.

DON'T IDLE AWAY Remember to turn your engine off when in a traffic jam, idling or waiting at a level crossing. An idling engine can produce up to twice the emissions of a car in motion.

Driving at 80kph (50mph) uses 30% less fuel than driving at 110kph (70mph).

For every 9,700km (6,000 miles) the average car travels, it generates its own weight in CO_2 emissions.

 A car travelling at 64kph (40mph) in fifth gear uses around 25% less fuel than one travelling at the same speed in third gear.

 There were just over 600 million private cars on the world's roads in 2007; it's predicted there'll be up to 2.7 billion by 2050.

Every litre (⅕ gallon) of petrol saved keeps 2kg (4lb) of CO_2 out of the atmosphere – so every increase in fuel efficiency makes a difference!

When just 1% of car owners properly maintain their vehicles, more than 400 million kg (880 million lb) of CO_2 is kept out of the atmosphere.

 In many countries, including the UK and the Netherlands, eco-driving now forms part of the theory section of driving tests. Driving this way increases fuel efficiency by 6% and saves each driver £100 a year in petrol.

LEADING BY EXAMPLE
Companies can do much to reduce the carbon footprint of their employees' journeys to and from work. Why not suggest the following strategies to your employer:
- run a car-share via the company intranet or a central bulletin board
- trade in the company car fleet for corporate membership of a car club
- offer incentives for low-carbon commuting, such as an extra day of annual leave.

Car club members drive 47% fewer miles each year than car owners.

CAR-SHARING AND CAR CLUBS

Try sharing a car or joining a car club rather than owning your own four wheels. You'll save money and hassle and cut your carbon footprint considerably.

NEIGHBOURLY SHARING If you get on well with your neighbours, try jointly owning and maintaining a car.

SHARE A LIFT TO WORK If everyone who regularly drives to work on their own shared a lift just once a week, traffic volumes would fall by 12–15%.

START A CARPOOL with friends or co-workers. Organize it yourself, or use a specialist website to link up with people doing similar journeys.

JOIN A CAR CLUB These operate in cities worldwide, providing self-service pay-as-you-go cars. You simply book a car by phone or via the Internet, use it for as long as you need, paying by the hour and/or km/mile, then leave it in a designated parking bay for the next user.

The average moving car in the EU contains only 1.2 people.

Every 1,600km (1,000 miles) you travel in an average-size petrol-fuelled family saloon (sedan) that does 15kpl (35mpg) causes 300kg (660lb) of CO_2 emissions.

The average Western commuter burns 1,290 litres (284 gallons) of fuel a year, creating a 3.4 tonne (7,500lb) cloud of CO_2. Joining a carpool can cut that figure by half or more.

The average American spends 18 cents of every dollar they earn on buying, running and maintaining cars.

If they average two car trips a week, the average UK citizen could save over £2,000 a year by trading in their car for a car club membership.

There are car clubs running in more than 600 cities worldwide.

In North America, priority lanes for vehicles occupied by two people or more are a common way to incentivize car-sharing.

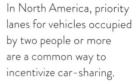

You can save a tonne (2,200lb) of CO_2 every year if your new car is just 0.9kpl (2mpg) more efficient than your current one.

A stop-start system, which switches off your car's engine whenever you stop and uses electricity from the battery to move forward again, can increase kpl/mpg by up to 15%.

Large SUVs (Sports Utility Vehicles) take 50% more energy to manufacture, and produce around 50% more CO_2 per km/mile than the average car.

CARS

When buying a new car, make sure that it's better for the environment than the last one. (And ask yourself whether you need a car at all ...)

CHOOSE THE SMALLEST CAR AND ENGINE that will meet your everyday needs. Look for the car with the lowest emissions in your chosen category, and save money on both fuel and tax.

BUY AN ELECTRIC CAR Electric cars produce half the CO_2 emissions of a diesel car, including the manufacturing emissions. When choosing an electric car, check if it is Next Green Car recommended (nextgreencar.com). You can also use the website to compare the charging times, costs and driving range of different electric cars. You should also consider whether the car's manufacturer has genuine plans to phase out diesel and electrify all new vehicles.

INVEST WISELY Unfortunately, electric cars still tend to cost more to buy and there are less available to purchase second-hand. Look for government grants and use the Next Green Car website to search for used electric cars for sale.

GREEN ENERGY Charge your electric car using 100% renewable energy from an ethical company. If you don't have suitable off-street parking at home, the number of public charging points are increasing, especially in cities; however, you will have less control over the energy supplier. As of March 2022, there are over 30,000 public charge points in the UK, which you can locate using the Zap Map (zap-map.com).

BEST OF BOTH WORLDS If possible, opt for a purely electric car. However, hybrid cars can be more affordable and can travel a longer range. If buying a hybrid, choose an electric motor with a petrol, rather than diesel, engine. Older hybrids use batteries to lower fuel consumption, whereas newer plug-in hybrids can be recharged like electric cars and travel 50–65km (30–40 miles) on battery alone.

CHOOSE A MODEL WITH A MANUAL GEARBOX If you follow the principles of eco driving (see pp.117–19), manual cars tend to be more fuel-efficient than automatic equivalents.

MINIMIZE ADD-ONS such as sat-nav systems – they can add to your car's weight and/or sap its battery, both of which lead to reduced fuel efficiency.

CO_2 emissions in the UK fell by roughly 10.7% in 2020, compared to 2019. Total greenhouse gas emissions dropped by 8.9%. This large fall is primarily due to the reduction in road transport and business operations during the COVID-19 lockdown.

In Norway Ultra Low Emission Vehicles accounted for over 45% of new vehicle sales in 2018, with the market share expected to reach 100% by 2025, thanks to incentives.

Air passengers carried (worldwide):

1985   0.9 billion

2005   2 billion

2025   4.5 billion (forecast)

In the UK, taking the train from London to Edinburgh produces one-seventh of the carbon emitted by flying.

Skipping just one 5-hour flight could cut your CO_2 emissions by a tonne (2,200lb), equivalent to 160 days of commuting 16km (10 miles) each way in a medium-sized car.

With proportionally more fuel used for take-off, the carbon footprint per passenger mile for short-haul flights is up to 25% larger than for long-haul flights.

A plane uses about as much fuel, and therefore produces about as much CO_2, as would every passenger on board driving their own car the same distance.

45% of air journeys in Europe are of 480km (300 miles) or less – well within the capabilities of a high-speed train.

Just 1% of the world's population cause half of the flying industry's carbon emissions, and 15% of the UK's population take 70% of flights.

Compare the costs, durations and impact of different travel options for any specific journey using the EcoPassenger website, (ecopassenger.org).

FLIGHT-FREE TRIPS

It's tough to swallow, but cutting out non-essential flights is one of the most important things you can do to reduce your carbon footprint.

👍 **EMBRACE THE ART OF SLOW TRAVEL** and treat the journey as part of the experience. Enjoy avoiding the hassles of security checks, in-flight inedibles and baggage reclaim, and on journeys of several hundred miles you'll probably find flight-free travel's quicker anyway!

👍 **GO BY RAIL** On average, trains emit two-thirds less CO_2 per passenger than planes.

👍 **TRAVEL ON A CARGO SHIP** You'll save money, visit places the average tourist never sees and dramatically slash your journey's carbon emissions. Or join the crew of a sailing boat for an invigorating, zero-carbon tour of the seas.

💲 **USE A COMPARISON WEBSITE** such as Skyscanner, which highlights lower-emission flights. Some airlines offer the option to offset your flight, and you can arrange this yourself. Make sure the scheme is traceable and verified. Remember that such schemes do not have immediate or guaranteed effects. Carbonfootprint.com helps you calculate your emissions and offset them.

WHY IS FLYING BAD FOR THE PLANET?

As well as releasing 2–3% of man-made CO_2 emissions, aviation contributes to the climate crisis by emitting nitrogen oxides, which form the greenhouse gas ozone. Because this happens at high altitude, the impact is magnified. Altogether the heating effect of air travel is 2.7 times greater than that of its CO_2 emissions alone, meaning that it is responsible for around 5% of global heating. Aviation is the fastest-growing source of man-made emissions, growing by around 5% a year, outstripping any efficiencies that can be achieved through improved technology. If it continues to grow at this rate, we'd have to eliminate emissions from almost all other sources to have a chance of achieving the reductions required to limit the climate crisis to 1.5°C above pre-industrial levels.

SUPPORT LOW-CARBON COMMUNITIES

Take inspiration from the many places around the world that are already moving toward low-carbon living. For example:

- Ashton Hayes in rural Cheshire, which is aiming to become England's first "carbon-neutral village"
- the growing network of "transition towns" such as Totnes in Devon, UK, which are actively trying to break their fossil-fuel dependency
- Boulder, Colorado, which in 2006 approved America's first "climate tax"
- Stockholm, Sweden, which is planning to become fossil fuel-free by 2040, with initiatives including biofuel-powered heating, renewably-fuelled buses and biogas-powered municipal vehicles
- in the UK, 802 communities are signed up as, or to become, Plastic-Free Communities, an initiative created by Surfers Against Sewage.

THE BIGGER PICTURE

To achieve the scale of change required at the pace necessary to avoid the worst impacts of the climate crisis will demand action at all levels of society.

 WRITE TO YOUR ELECTED REPRESENTATIVE to express your support for legislative change that speeds up the transition to a low-carbon society.

 VOTE FOR THE PARTY with the strongest commitment to tackling the climate crisis.

GET LOCALLY ACTIVE Petition for change in your local government and get involved in one of the environmental groups in your area.

 CONVINCE A SCEPTIC Fighting to reduce your own carbon footprint is good; persuading others to do the same is even better.

JOIN A NON-GOVERNMENTAL ORGANIZATION (NGO) that's campaigning for action to address the climate crisis.

SPEND YOUR MONEY WISELY Choose independent and ethical companies for all purchases and investments. Ask yourself whether businesses indirectly use your money to harm the planet.

Rising seas will put an estimated 70 million African lives at risk of flooding by 2080, displacing the people least responsible for the climate crisis.

 Just 100 companies' actions are the source of 71% of all global greenhouse gas emissions.

 74% of all local authorities in the UK have declared a climate emergency (as of summer 2021). What action has yours taken?

New investments in renewable energy could create 3.3 million jobs worldwide in the next 10 years.

 Recognizing that cities generate 80% of CO_2 emissions, the world's largest cities have formed a group called C40 to tackle the climate crisis.

81% of people agree that the COVID-19 pandemic shows the importance of protecting and restoring nature. And 76% believe that nature can contribute to economic recovery by helping reduce the risk of challenges such as flooding, unpredictable water supplies, and future pandemics.

FURTHER READING AND USEFUL WEBSITES

FURTHER READING

Berners-Lee, Mike, *How Bad are Bananas?: The carbon footprint of everything*, Profile Books, 2020

Extinction Rebellion, *This Is Not a Drill: The Extinction Rebellion Handbook*, Penguin, 2019

Grose, Anouchka, *A Guide to Eco-Anxiety: How to Protect the Planet and Your Mental Health*, Watkins Publishing, 2020

Hopkins, Rob, *From What Is to What If: Unleashing the Power of Imagination to Create the Future We Want*, Chelsea Green Publishing, 2020

McCallum, Will, *How to Give Up Plastic: A Guide to Changing the World, One Plastic Bottle at a Time*, Penguin Life, 2018

Morgan, Sally and Stoddart, Kim, *The Climate Change Garden*, Green Rocket, 2019

Tout, Ellen, *The Complete Book of Vegan Compleating: An A–Z of Zero-Waste Eating For the Mindful Vegan*, Nourish Books, 2021

Wilson-Powell, Georgina, *Is It Really Green?: Everyday Eco Dilemmas Answered*, Dorling Kindersley, 2021

USEFUL WEBSITES

GENERAL INFORMATION AND ADVICE

Earthwatch Institute (www.earthwatch.org)

The Ecologist online magazine (www.theecologist.org)

Friends of the Earth (www.foe.co.uk)

Global Action Plan (www.globalactionplan.org.uk)

Greenpeace (www.greenpeace.org.uk)

Pebble magazine (www.pebblemag.com)

The Intergovernmental Panel on Climate Change (www.ipcc.ch)

Royal Society for the Protection of Birds (www.rspb.org.uk)

The Climate Coalition (www.theclimatecoalition.org)

CARBON FOOTPRINT CALCULATORS
Carbon Footprint (www.carbonfootprint.com)
World Wildlife Fund (www.footprint.wwf.org.uk)

CHILDREN
Eco-Schools (www.eco-schools.org.uk)
National Association of Toy and Leisure Libraries (www.natll.org.uk)

ENERGY-SAVING ADVICE AND PRODUCTS
Centre for Alternative Technology (www.cat.org.uk)
Energy Saving Trust (www.est.org.uk)
Make My Money Matter (www.makemymoneymatter.co.uk)
ShareAction (www.shareaction.org)
Pawprint app (www.pawprint.eco)

GARDENING
The RHS (www.rhs.org.uk)
Garden Organic (www.gardenorganic.org.uk)
Vegan Organic Network (www.veganorganic.net)
Permaculture Association (www.permaculture.org.uk)

FOOD AND DRINK
The Soil Association (www.soilassociation.org)
Sustain (www.sustainweb.org)
The Vegetarian Society (www.vegsoc.org)
The Vegan Society (www.vegansociety.com)
The Food Foundation (www.foodfoundation.org.uk)
Pesticide Action Network (www.pan-uk.org)

RENEWABLE ENERGY SUPPLIERS
Ecotricity (www.ecotricity.co.uk)
Good Energy (www.goodenergy.co.uk)
Green Power (www.greenpower.gov.au)
Energy Saving Trust (energysavingtrust.org.uk)

SHOPPING
Buy Me Once (www.buymeonce.com)
Buy Nothing Day (www.buynothingday.co.uk)
Craigslist (www.craigslist.co.uk)
Freecycle (www.freecycle.org)
Gumtree (www.gumtree.co.uk)
TRAID – Textile Reuse and International Development (www.traid.org.uk)
Ethical Consumer (www.ethicalconsumer.org)

TRANSPORT
Cyclists' Touring Club (www.ctc.org.uk)
Sustainable Travel International (www.sustainabletravel.org)
Sustrans (www.sustrans.org.uk)
Transport 2000 (www.transport2000.org.uk)

WASTE
Waste Resources Action Plan (www.wrap.org.uk)
Wastewatch (www.wastewatch.org.uk)

PLASTIC
Marine Conservation Society (www.mcsuk.org)
Sea Shepherd (www.seashepherd.org.uk)
Ocean Conservancy (www.oceanconservancy.org)
The 2 Minute Foundation (www.2minute.org)
Surfers Against Sewage (www.sas.org.uk)
Plastic Soup Foundation (www.plasticsoupfoundation.org)
Refill (www.refill.org.uk)

INDEX

ACKNOWLEDGEMENTS

Thank you to Ella Chappell, my wonderful commissioning editor at Watkins Books, firstly for taking a chance on my debut book, and secondly, for giving me the opportunity to work on this book. And thanks to the team at Watkins.

My thanks also go to Joanna Yarrow, who wrote and researched the first edition of this book. Much has changed since its publication in 2008, so I must also thank the many organisations (some of which are listed in the further reading section) whose vital research and knowledge helped inform the advice and statistics in these pages.

Thank you to my partner Nadia, who I am so proud to know, and who always supports me, helps fine-tune my copy, and knows where to buy the best vegan wine after a day of writing. And thanks, of course, to my dog Bella who keeps me company while I work.

I would also like to share my thanks for anyone who has supported my debut book, *The Complete Book of Vegan Compleating*. It has been so lovely to meet people, hear about recipes you have made and see more people inspired by compleating.

A huge thanks also to you – for reading this book and for taking steps to make a difference, and to each of the amazing people doing the same.